Cooking Vegetarian

Healthy, Delicious, and
Easy Vegetarian Cuisine

Vesanto Melina, R.D.

Joseph Forest

D0721694

CHRONIMED PUBLISHING

Cooking Vegetarian: Healthy, Delicious, and Easy
Vegetarian Cooking © 1998 by Vesanto Melina, R.D.,
and Joseph Forest

Originally published in Canada by Macmillan Canada,
1996

Library of Congress Cataloging-in-Publication Data
Melina, Vesanto, R.D., and Joseph Forest
Cooking Vegetarian by Vesanto Melina, R.D., and
Joseph Forest

       p.   cm.

Includes index.

ISBN 1-56561-172-1; $18.95

Acquiring Editor: Cheryl Kimball
Copy Editor: Jolene Steffer
Art/Production Manager: Claire Lewis
Text Design & Production: David Enyeart
Cover Design: Counterpunch

Printed in Canada.

Published by
Chronimed Publishing
P.O. Box 59032
Minneapolis, MN 55459-0032

10   9   8   7   6   5   4   3   2   1

Contents

To David Melina, thank you for your clear and steadfast vision, your integrity, and for sharing my life journey.

And to Dr. Michael Klaper and Dr. Neal Barnard, two physicians who inspire me with their blending of scientific expertise, integrity, and ethics.

VESANTO

To the Living Spirit of Truth, who blesses the vision of three great medical giants: Dr. Deepak Chopra, Dr. Dean Ornish, and Dr. Andrew Weil

JOSEPH

Acknowledgments

Our deepest thanks to David Melina for patient and precise assistance with the nutritional analysis, for computer expertise, for valuable feedback, for making such great salads, and for testing up to six salad dressings at a time with his meals. Thanks to Debrah Rafel for her editing, assistance in developing and evaluating recipes, and for her love, support, and friendship during the creation of the Canadian edition.

Much love to our dear friends who supported the vision in a myriad of ways: Michael Fisher, chef and colleague, for his suggestions and recipe contributions; Lance Shaler for his valuable insight; and Jean-Pierre and Kate Ross LeBlanc for their suggestions.

We would like to extend our appreciation to our skillful editors at Chronimed Publishing—especially Cheryl Kimball and David Enyeart—and to the staff at Macmillan Canada for their expertise and vision in creating the original Canadian edition of this book.

We are grateful to the registered dietitians who unfailingly offered us their expertise and provided invaluable assistance when asked: Suzanne Havala, Ginny and Mark Messina, Reed Mangels, Carollyne Conlinn, Brenda Davis, Victoria Harrison, and Jean Fremont. We're also grateful to Sharon Denny on the Public Education Team at the American Dietetic Association in Oak Park, Chicago, for feedback on the Vegetarian Food Guide.

For thoughtful assistance with chapters 1 and 2: Al and Shirley Hunting and Carol Sue Janes, who assisted with the text for the organic foods section, Jean Vignes for her poetic contribution, Donna Jenkins for assistance with editing, and Gaby Brahney for her assistance with the index.

Many thanks to those who provided assistance in recipe testing and development: Valerie McIntyre, Michelle Jenkins, Shui Ing Lim, Carol Sue and Francis Janes, Bianca Molinari, Georgina Seifert, Nancy and Paul Travis, Delta Nutrition Systems, Junko Valle of Chicago, Sheila

Hoffman, Debra Gallie, and Elysa Markowitz. Thanks to Bhora Derry for her love of cooking healthy food and to members of Windsong co-housing community for evaluation of recipes.

Thanks to the following authors and friends who allowed us to use recipes from their books: Rynn Berry, author of *Famous Vegetarians and Their Favorite Recipes,* 1996, and *Food for the Gods, Vegetarianism and the World's Religions,* 1998 (Pythagorean Publishers); Ron Pickarski, author of *Friendly Foods,* 1991, and *Eco-Cuisine,* 1995 (Ten Speed Press); Joanne Stepaniak, author of *Vegan Vittles,* 1996, *The Nutritional Yeast Cookbook,* 1997 (The Book Publishing Company), and *The Sourcebook of Vegan Living,* 1998 (Lowell House), plus books listed on page 232; and Mollie Katzen, author of *The Moosewood Cookbook,* 1977 (Ten Speed Press).

We are grateful to those who generously provided outstanding products for recipe testing: Dwayne and Doreen Smith of GrainWorks Inc.; Sally Gralla, Mary Scott, and Cristin Colling of Eden Foods; Kelly Smith of Frontier Herbs; Tom McReynolds of Morinauga Foods; Aaran Stevens and Tamara Sawall of Nature's Path Foods; Omega Nutrition Canada; Sunrise Soya Foods; Yves Potvin of Yves Veggie Cuisine; Red Star Nutritional Yeast/Universal Foods; and Jerry Duncan, Lorne Broten, Don Coggins, George Conquergood, Dusty Cunningham, Ron Upton, and Kathleen Lee at ProSoya Foods Incorporated. Thanks to David Westcott for assistance with recipe analysis and to Jae Choi in connection with the outstanding Green Power Juicer.

We appreciate the fine technical support and service provided by ESHA research staff in connection with the excellent Food Processor nutritional analysis program: Patrick Murphy, Elizabeth Hands, Robert Geltz, Layne Westover, Alicia Teem, and David Hands.

Sincere thanks to everyone who made the photography for the book possible: Larry Nowakowski and R. Steve Martin of Universal Foods; Diane Jang and Peter Joe of Sunrise Soya Foods; Sally Gralla of Eden Foods; Robert Gaffney and Amber Hall of Omega Nutrition Canada; Adonis Photography; Belinda Wheatley, food stylist; Ross Durant Photography; the B.C. Blueberry Council; Laurie Jones of Whalebone Production; and Al Reid, photographer.

Special thanks to: Michael Theodore and Gail Mountain for their assistance with the appendix.

For their inspiration and help, we thank: Graham Kerr and his associates Karin Rowles and dietitian Kristine Duncan; Ron Pickarski and Nancy Loving of Eco-Cuisine. For Vesanto's opportunity to participate as a staff dietitian in the "Open Your Heart" retreats, we thank Dr. Dean Ornish and the dietitians, staff, and chef Jean-Marc Fullsack of the Preventive Medicine Research Institute.

We also offer our heartfelt appreciation and thanks to: Dr. E.S. Goranson, Vesanto's father, an outstanding teacher and scientist; Aldona Goranson, Vesanto's stepmother, a wonderful cook and deeply inspiring woman; and Louise Forest, Joseph's mother, for her unconditional love and patience.

Foreword by Graham Kerr

Please do me a favor and spend a few minutes going through this book: read recipe headings and stop briefly to look at the authors' personal comments that introduce each dish. Please do that before you read on…

…Thank you! That's the way to get the "flavor" and the passion of these two special people—Vesanto Melina and Joseph Forest. Are you, after that swift survey, just a little hungry? I should hope so, because this is *real* food.

Clearly, if you know anything of my career, I'm not a vegetarian; however, I am on a journey toward that "promised land." At this time, I can best describe myself as a cooperative traffic cop. Imagine me at a favorite four-way intersection. I have no gun or tickets, not even a whistle to blow. Since there are no street signs and I have a perpetually pleasant smile (the metaphor more than the reality!), folks stop to ask their way.

"I'm well, but I don't want to get sick," some tell me. I direct them to the right. "That's the road to prevention," I tell them. "Mostly plant foods with less than 20 percent of calories from fat."

"I'm sick and I want to be well," explains another group. "Try the road to reversal," I suggest. "That's vegan/vegetarian, with about 10 percent of calories from fat."

There are other folks on the road who want to know how to care for those they love. Basically, I keep on sending them left and right. Occasionally, a fourth kind yells, "Get out of my way; I'm coming straight through!" I don't have any means to ticket them; it's not really my task. But before long, these apparently carefree consumers may spot a sign reading "Dead End" and they'll either turn around and ask for directions or they'll drive right over the edge.

Where do you fit in? Well? Sick? Or do you love someone and want the best for them? Every word you read in this book will give you greater power to make whole-mind decisions about your future health.

I'm totally convinced, from over 24 years of study, that the more plant life you consume, the healthier you will become, and even more wonderful, the more you will enjoy the food you prepare. This is my 50th year earning a living in the food business. For 26 of those years, my career choice was in what I call "mural" foods— —no frames, no limits, just whatever turned on the taste buds.

I ate that way and I fed my wife Treena that way. Her cholesterol built to 360, mine to 265. Treena eventually suffered a stroke and heart attack when she was 53. I had gout and passed kidney stones when I was 35! Fortunately, life conspired to give us wake-up calls while there was still time to make a turn and ask for directions.

Today, it's our 11th year of major change. Treena's cholesterol is down to 180 (105 LDL) and mine is 160 (110 LDL) Treena's hypertension is under control (126/84). Her Type 2 diabetes is under control and she has no need of the once-proposed heart bypass operation. There have been lots of changes. We've exercised (within reason), enjoyed friendships, taken real time for spiritual reflection and action. We've set goals and included those we respect in "accountability loops" to help us on our way. At every turn, there's been plant life. Sure we've met cattle crossings. Still do, but more and more we walk through fields where the only thing that's organic is the soil.

Finally, let me add a brief word about world hunger. I've been heavily involved in this issue since my conversion to Christianity in March 1974. It was at this time that I became available enough to really hear that "once every three-quarters of every second, a child under the age of five dies because of malnutrition-assisted disease." Compare that to the frequency with which we currently die (in North America alone) from unwise eating. That number is currently once in every 105 seconds.

Clearly this is a moral issue that transcends the religious. All of us can feel the pain, on both sides. Treena and I changed that pain into a purpose. We reduced our addictive response to meat products and cut out $1,000 a year on our food budget. Half of these savings went back into the coffers to increase vegetable purchases and the other half went to support two at-risk children in Ethiopia and Brazil. We benefited hugely and so do they; in a totally microscopic way. The world is a better place and it is plants and people that make that possible.

Introduction by Ron Pickarski

"Nothing will benefit human health and increase the chances for survival of life on earth as much as the evolution to a vegetarian diet."
—Albert Einstein

Twenty years ago vegetarian diets weren't readily accepted in the dietetic community as being nutritionally balanced. Moreover, professional chefs looked at vegetarianism with indifference. Times and diets have changed, though, with the advance of nutritional/medical research into the effects of diet on chronic degenerative diseases. In recent years, the findings have revolutionized attitudes of Americans toward the impact of diet on health. The value of a vegetarian diet has emerged as a direct dietary solution, in part, to most chronic degenerative diseases in America.

Increasing numbers of Americans are aware of the roles diet plays in total health, as well as the high cost of health care. These factors are major incentives for making the transition to vegetarianism. Americans spent $600 billion, 12 percent of the Gross National Product, on health care in 1990. Health insurance companies in America realize that preventive medicine such as Dr. Dean Ornish's low-fat vegetarian heart reversal

Ron Pickarski (formerly Brother Ron) is the first professional vegetarian chef to be certified as an Executive Chef by the American Culinary Federation. His interest in cooking and eating healthier foods began in 1976 when he was suffering from ill health and weighed 200 pounds, at a height of 5' 8". Ron was inspired to work in the kitchen at the friary in order to have access to creating healthier foods for himself. He soon became a vegetarian and later a professional chef and has easily maintained his weight at 130 pounds ever since. Ron's specialty is gourmet vegetarian cuisine prepared with plant-based foods. He is the founder/director of the American Natural Foods Team which competes at the quadrennial International Culinary Olympics in Germany. Between 1980 and 1996 he won seven medals (gold, silver, and bronze) with plant-based foods and was the first chef in the history of that prestigious event to do so. Ron is the author of two cookbooks: *Eco-Cuisine: An Ecological Approach to Gourmet Vegetarian Cooking* and *Friendly Foods: Gourmet Vegetarian Cuisine* (Ten Speed Press, Berkeley, CA, 1995, 1991).

program, is an economical, effective strategy that costs far less than a $50,000 open heart operation. These companies are opting to cover preventive approaches for high-risk patients, as opposed to traditional therapy.

I always recommend investing in pure, high quality foods and taking time to exercise and reduce stress as a preventive measure, rather than paying the extremely high cost of health care due to poor health and disease. The economic advantages of a vegetarian diet are even more evident when you consider that the same amount of money will buy more than 56 grams of top quality protein from soybeans and only 10 grams from beef—even with all the subsidies supporting the meat industry! Clearly, the vegetarian diet is a win/win situation for consumers and insurance companies.

In Eastern philosophy it is believed that the larger the front the larger the back, or simply translated, all good has a dark side. Scientific research, while enlightening humanity as to diet's role in health, has created confusion for the health-seeking consumer. The confusion comes from mixed messages from the scientific and pseudo-scientific community. The T-Factor diet, for instance, advocates a high complex carbohydrate diet while the Zone Diet advocates more protein and fat, and less carbohydrates. Many Americans are confused by all the dietary misinformation and are waiting for valid scientific information from which to base their dietary change. The one dietary approach that has sound scientific validity and is gaining momentum in America is vegetarianism.

The vegetarian diet has been confirmed through many independent studies such as the China Health Project, Dr. Dean Ornish's research, and J.A. Scharffenberg's research in applied nutrition at Loma Linda University. It is clearly a balanced diet that also has a positive impact on our economic and environmental health. So strong is the vegetarian movement that in 1993, former Secretary of Agriculture Mike Espy called upon the USDA to fulfill its educational mission by providing consumers with information on vegetarian diets. There were 12.5 million adult vegetarians in 1993, twice the number for 1985, and the numbers continue to increase.

Food is the most intimate relationship you has with yourself. It reflects your cultural, social, economic, and spiritual upbringing. Vesanto

Melina and Joseph Forest, in *Cooking Vegetarian,* lay a simple foundation for the inspired soul to make this transformation to a healthy vegetarian diet with simply presented professional dietary advice and wonderful recipes. Together, with their years of experience in pioneering vegetarian nutrition and cuisine, they provide a sound starting point to begin the transition to vegetarianism. The aesthetics of food and the chemistry of nutrition must be understood and married. Vesanto and Joseph successfully accomplish this task while cultivating the health of the seeker's mind.

RON PICKARSKI, CEC, PRESIDENT
AND EXECUTIVE CHEF/CONSULTANT,
ECO-CUISINE, INC.
BOULDER, COLORADO
MARCH 1998

Two Words from the Authors

A word from Vesanto

It is indeed an honor to address you, the reader, in the company of these two giants, Graham Kerr and Ron Pickarski. The recipes that follow are the culmination of a vision I had in the early '80s of playing a part in a dietary shift of America. I imagined working alongside those who had stepped out to take leadership roles in this enormous task.

Like these chefs, I evolved from a traditional diet, heavy on the meat, potatoes, and dairy. The influencing thought of the 1940s and '50s (my childhood and adolescence) was about "getting enough"—enough protein, enough vitamins, enough calories. In fact, in the '30s and '40s, fat and sugar were entire food groups on the food guide! I trusted the scientific thinking of this era for many years. After all, why wouldn't I? My father was an outstanding physiologist in his own right. He did graduate work with Best and Banting, who discovered insulin and led in diabetes research. My father later studied cancer, though his research focused on test tubes and lab animals, rather than lifestyles.

Another influence was my mother, who created cookie parties with all the neighborhood children for my early birthday celebrations, and made life a great deal of fun in many ways. My parents led to my appreciation of two facets of nutrition: the academic and the appetizing. It wasn't until later that the links between food choices and other aspects of life fell into place.

After the birth of my children, I had the opportunity to teach at a university, live on an immense cattle ranch, travel around the world several times, and live in India and Nepal for four years. During these years I learned a great deal about the production and preparation of food in our and other cultures, and the seeds were planted for the vegetarian ways of eating that I have followed since 1978.

My initial attraction to a vegetarian diet was enjoyment of the food itself, shared with people in many parts of the globe. My daughter, Kavyo, has been a lifelong vegetarian and my son, Xoph, began cooking early and developed a fine sense of the use of spices and seasonings. Food preparation has long been a comforting and creative solitary activity, as well as a pleasurable way to spend time in the kitchen with family and friends.

Over time, the profound effects of our food choices on the environment, health, human hunger, and the lives of animals have led me to make vegetarian nutrition and foods central to my professional career. In doing the extensive research for my first book, *Becoming Vegetarian,* (published by The Book Publishing Company, 1995) I came to see that not only could we get all the nutrients we need in a plant-based diet, but that such a diet makes sense for reasons that become more significant for me each month. My own way of eating has become totally plant-based (vegan), further inspired and supported by David Melina. My gradual transition over the years gave me an understanding of the challenges and solutions for people everywhere on the continuum between near-vegetarian through to vegan.

I have seen a shift in attitude among those at the forefront of the dietetics profession, from an earlier attitude that vegetarian diets are nutritionally risky, to an awareness that greater risks of chronic disease are associated with the heavy meat- and dairy-centered diets of most North Americans. Several years ago, I had the honor of receiving the prestigious Clintec award for leadership in dietetics, due in part to my vegetarian expertise.

Executive chef Ron Pickarski was described to me with great enthusiasm ten years ago by Joseph Forest. Ron became a legend for his pioneering work with plant-based food presentations at the Culinary Olympics in Germany. He has won several medals, competing against classic meat- and dairy-based cuisine. At the 1993 annual Festival of the American Vegan Society*, I was privileged to finally meet Ron Pickarski and to sample the outstanding fare he provides for these events each year. In September of 1997, Ron received the ultimate honor at the Culinary Olympics—a gold medal.

*For References and Resources, see page 231.

One day in 1997 I had a call on my Seattle phone line. "Hello, this is Graham Kerr, and I wondered if you would be willing to let us include your book, *Becoming Vegetarian,* in our resource catalog." Would I! We proceeded to talk for an hour and I was deeply touched by this man who is so moved by the energy of the heart and by a concern for the human hunger in the world.

It is truly a gift for a dietitian to collaborate with chefs, and I am grateful indeed! Once I teamed up with my coauthor, the sensory appeal of the food I create took a quantum leap, and "delicious" took on new meaning. Joseph has been a wonderful teacher for me, as well as a truly inspirational human being.

A word from Joseph

From a very early age I have been mysteriously drawn to food. As a young teenager living at home, I watched *The Galloping Gourmet,* hosted by Graham Kerr, at every opportunity. Impressions obviously ran deep—I became a professional chef. Years later Graham is back in my life, this time to write the foreword to the U.S. edition of *Cooking Vegetarian.* I am absolutely thrilled.

My first formal experience with food began at the young age of 13. I worked part time as a baker's assistant for three years. Although, at 16, the thought of a career in the arena of food was not a consideration, it seemed that this destiny would continue to draw me forward.

When I was 17, my father died of a massive heart attack. Although a crippling industrial accident certainly contributed to his untimely death, his diet most certainly played a major role. For years I had watched him ignore his doctor's advice against the consumption of certain foods. When reminded of this at home by my mother, he would act as though he knew better and shrug off any sense of danger. His premature death at the age of 50 had a very significant impact on me. Having witnessed the correlation between diet and disease, I began to investigate the other side of the coin—the healing power of foods.

My inquiry eventually led to formal chef training. I initially enrolled to deepen my understanding of food and to improve my cooking skills. However, by the time I graduated I had acknowledged my strong intuitive gift with food and only then did I decide to embark upon a career as a professional chef in fine restaurants and hotels.

During the course of my career, I often contemplated my father's death. At work my duties involved preparing and serving many of the rich and fatty foods my father had been advised to reduce or eliminate. I knew in my heart that I was contributing to the health problems of the nation, yet I couldn't ignore my deep love of food. This created a discrepancy in my life until I eventually left the restaurant and hotel industry to explore and work with foods I believed would have a more beneficial impact on my body and the planet.

Soon after leaving the Four Seasons Hotel kitchen I met Vesanto Melina and together we developed a series of vegetarian cooking classes. She offered nutritional knowledge and I led the hands-on cooking portion of the class. We taught hundreds of individuals—from teenagers to grandmothers. Fun was had by all and our students went home richer for the experience.

During this transition time, executive chef Ron Pickarski's vegetarian cookbooks caught my attention. He had participated several times at the prestigious Culinary Art Olympics, held every four years in Frankfurt, Germany. Master chefs from around the globe painstakingly compete for bronze, silver, and gold medals by artistically preparing incredibly elaborate platters of food. This is culinary art at its highest level. What impressed me about Ron was that his work was entirely plant-based and he was winning medals for his imaginative efforts. Congratulations! His work continues to inspire me and I am very grateful and honored for the introduction he has written for this book.

Over the many years that I have worked with natural whole foods, three personal perspectives have emerged.

1. Transition from one dietary lifestyle to another can take years. For lasting results, this important process requires time and patience.

2. Since each person is constitutionally different, no single diet can be applied to everyone. Although we all need carbohydrates, protein, vitamins, and minerals, the combinations of foods we choose in the process of meeting those needs are as varied as there are people on earth. This process also changes from one stage of life to another.

3. We are all brilliantly-tailored individuals, guided by a deep source of inner intelligence. If we pay attention to the wisdom of this intelligence we will be led into the dietary pattern that best serves who we are as individuals.

The recipes in this book were developed according to the tastes and preferences of the authors. It is our sincere wish that you will derive joy from them in good health. As you work with and adapt this book to suit your lifestyle, be prepared to learn, eat, enjoy, and laugh.

Chapter One

Healthy, Delicious, and Easy

The scrumptious aroma of potatoes baking in the oven on a cold winter afternoon.

Black bean soup simmering on the stove, with the scents of onion, oregano, and cumin wafting upwards from the pot.

The youthful green of lightly steamed broccoli, the glistening red of sweet bell peppers, the sunshine yellow of crunchy corn.

Your first mouthful of a toasted sandwich heaped with slices of fresh tomato and avocado.

The explosion of flavor awakening your senses when you bite into a warm cranberry pecan muffin.

Oh, the pleasures of savory food. When it comes to great nutrition, are you accustomed to thinking that if it's nutritious, it probably doesn't taste good? You'll be delighted to discover that nothing could be further from the truth. As our food awareness increases, we are compelled to leave aside those fat- and cholesterol-laden foods that are so aptly described as "a heart attack on a plate." We're looking for a marriage of flavor along with high-quality ingredients. That's exactly what recipes in this book provide.

In the creative collaboration of the authors, the words "healthy," "delicious," and "easy" have been central themes for the foods we prepare. These three words have been both a challenge and an inspiration. Recipes have had to qualify on all three counts. Our vision has been to create appetizing and nourishing dishes that can be assembled by people with full and busy lives.

In this chapter, we introduce the nutritional guidelines that serve as the foundation for the menus and recipes that follow. The Vegetarian Food Guide on page 23 was modeled after national food guides developed by dietitians and other nutritional experts in the United States, Canada, Great Britain, Australia, and New Zealand. It retains the strengths of these national food guides and provides a solid basis for planning your plant-based diet, menus, and shopping lists. For more detailed nutrition information and specific guidelines for pregnancy and infancy through adolescence, see *Becoming Vegetarian,* by dietitians Vesanto Melina, Brenda Davis, and Victoria Harrison, published by The Book Publishing Company, 1995. To quote the *Journal of the American Dietetic Association,* "Few books on vegetarian nutrition are as comprehensive and accurate as *Becoming Vegetarian.*"*

The Vegetarian Food Guide supports you in getting all the nutrients you need for great health. Nutrients are food components that help nourish the body. That is, they provide energy, serve as building materials, maintain or repair the body, and support growth. Nutrients include protein (with nine essential amino acids), carbohydrate, essential fatty acids, 13 vitamins, more than 16 minerals, and water. In the Guide, similar foods—that is foods high in many of the same nutrients—are grouped together. Foods are divided into the following five categories beginning at the base of the pyramid:

- ◆ Bread, Cereal, Grains & Pasta Group
- ◆ Vegetables Group
- ◆ Fruits Group
- ◆ Milk & Alternatives Group
- ◆ Beans & Alternatives Group

*Journal of the American Dietetic Association, May 1996, pages 531–2.

The Vegetarian Food Guide

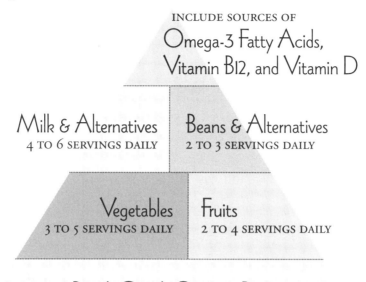

INCLUDE SOURCES OF
Omega-3 Fatty Acids, Vitamin B12, and Vitamin D

Milk & Alternatives
4 TO 6 SERVINGS DAILY

Beans & Alternatives
2 TO 3 SERVINGS DAILY

Vegetables
3 TO 5 SERVINGS DAILY

Fruits
2 TO 4 SERVINGS DAILY

Bread, Cereal, Grains & Pasta
6 TO 11 SERVINGS DAILY

Serving Sizes

From the pyramid tip…

OMEGA-3 FATTY ACIDS
1 tsp. flaxseed oil; 1 Tbsp. canola oil; 6 oz. firm tofu; 1/4 cup walnuts
VITAMIN B12 *(see page 33)*
VITAMIN D *(see page 34)*

Milk & Alternatives Group

4 TO 6 SERVINGS DAILY
1 cup cooked or 2 cups raw broccoli, bok choy, kale, okra, or napa cabbage; fortified beverages, tofu, or other foods providing ≥15% of the DV for calcium; 3–4 Tbsp. almonds or almond butter; 5 figs; 1 Tbsp. blackstrap molasses; 1/3 cup dried hijiki seaweed; 1 cup cooked black or white beans; 1/2 cup milk or yogurt; 3/4 oz. cheese

Beans & Alternatives Group

2 TO 3 SERVINGS DAILY
1 cup cooked beans, peas, or lentils; 1/2 cup firm tofu or tempeh; 1 patty of meat analogues; 1/4 cup nuts, seeds, or their butters; 2 cups soy milk; 2 eggs

Vegetables Group

3 TO 5 SERVINGS DAILY
1/2 cup fresh, frozen, or cooked vegetable; 1 medium vegetable (e.g. potato or carrot); 1 cup salad; 3/4 cup vegetable juice

Fruits Group

2 TO 4 SERVINGS DAILY
1/2 cup fresh, frozen, or cooked fruit; 1 medium fruit; 2 small fruits (e.g., apricot, plum); 3/4 cup fruit juice; 1/4 cup dried fruit

Bread, Cereal, Grains, & Pasta Group

6 TO 11 SERVINGS DAILY
1 slice bread, small roll, biscuit, tortilla, chapati, roti, bannock, or scone; 1/2 large bun, bagel, pita bread, or English muffin; 1/2 cup cooked cereal; 1 oz. ready-to-eat cereal; 2 Tbsp. wheat germ; 1/2 cup cooked grain or pasta; 1 small (or 1/2 large) pancake, waffle, or muffin; 2 large (or 4 small) crackers

At the tip of the pyramid is reference to Vitamins D and B12 and omega-3 fatty acids, which are referred to in more detail on pages 32 through 34. An additional category, not included in the guide, is Extras, the foods that are high in fat or sugar or have little nutritional merit, such as commercial cakes and pastries. (In contrast, the desserts in this book are delicious, yet they are made with a high proportion of nourishing ingredients from the food groups.)

Diets consumed by vegetarians range from lacto-ovo-vegetarian (including dairy products and eggs) to vegan (foods of plant origin only), with many variations. Our objective here is to provide a sound nutritional framework that can be adapted for a wide range of vegetarian food patterns. Whatever your dietary choice, it is important to select from all of the food groups, because each group is particularly rich in certain nutrients and poor in others. If you eat meat, fish, and poultry, count a 2- to 3-ounce portion as a serving from the Beans & Alternatives Group.

In practice, the system becomes marvelously simple. Just select a few foods from each group over the course of a day to meet the recommended number of servings. If you select wisely, even your snacks and desserts will provide valuable contributions to your daily needs. The guide is for a typical day's intake; however, it needn't be followed rigidly—selections can be averaged over a few days. People with small body sizes, sedentary lifestyles, and small appetites can choose the minimum number of servings from each category and larger or more active people the upper end of the range (or more).

Similarities and differences within each food group

While foods within a particular food group have similarities in their concentrations of minerals, vitamins, protein, and carbohydrate, the nutritional profile of each food has unique features. To illustrate this, foods in the Beans & Alternatives Group have significant amounts of protein, iron, zinc, magnesium, and certain B vitamins, yet foods within this group can vary markedly in other components. For example, lentils, peas, and most beans provide plenty of protein and trace minerals, yet they are spectacularly low in fat. In lentils, only 3 percent of the calories come from the plant oils present (page 27). These legumes are valuable additions to a weight-loss, heart-healthy, or diabetic diet because they contribute a great deal nutritionally and help keep your blood sugar level.

Soybeans differ from most other beans in that they contain a substantial proportion of fat—9 percent of cooked soybeans by weight or 42 percent of calories. The oil present in soy is beneficial. Soybeans provide both of the essential fatty acids, linoleic acid (an omega-6 fatty acid) and linolenic acid (an omega-3 fatty acid) in a good ratio of 7:1. The World Health Organization recommends a ratio between 5:1 and 10:1 for the overall diet. We require these essential fatty acids for building cell membranes and for important hormone-like substances that regulate body function. Soybeans also contain isoflavones, which are strong antioxidants and mild plant estrogens. Extensive research shows that soyfoods protect us in a number of ways against heart disease and certain types of cancer.

Within the same Beans & Alternatives Group, you'll find nuts, seeds, and their butters. These foods, while much higher in fat and lower in protein than legumes, offer numerous health benefits. They contain monounsaturated fats (the valuable components of fats found in olive oil), vitamin E, trace minerals and fiber. These fats do not appear to pose the same health risks as trans fatty acids and animal fats. In moderation, nut and seed butters are important in the diets of growing children, teens, and adults with high energy needs. For additional benefit, if you choose almonds, you'll be getting a calcium-rich food; if you munch on cashews, you'll obtain plenty of zinc, and fresh walnuts are an excellent source of omega-3 fatty acids. Most people will benefit from the addition of a few nuts or seeds to granola or a salad. Since a cup of nuts provides 800 calories and over 70 grams of fat, you'll probably want to use them as a condiment, rather than eating a whole bowl!

So, choose an average of two servings from the Beans & Alternatives Group daily, and vary your choices. Variety in all the food groups will make your meals interesting and help you get all the nutrients you need.

Complementary protein: theme from a bygone era

In the early 1970s, protein complementation (the careful combining of grains and legumes to ensure intake of all essential amino acids) was considered a necessary part of vegetarian meal planning. This concept, now outdated, was based on animal research that underestimated the nutritional value of plant protein for humans. Subsequent research has clearly demonstrated that when we take in sufficient calories and consume an assortment of the foods shown in the Vegetarian Food Guide, we get all the amino acids needed to build top-quality protein. You can continue to eat that savory pea soup with fresh bread, sweet and sour tofu with steaming rice, or chili with cornbread, but enjoy these foods because they're delightful together, not because you need to combine the plant proteins at the same meal!

When you make your selections within each food group, you'll find that there can be quite a range in quality. As much as possible, choose fresh foods that have been minimally processed and grown without harmful pesticides, and prepare them in ways that help to preserve their nutrients.

Bread, Cereals, Grains & Pasta Group: the energy foods

The foods in this group are central to your energy supply. Grains are parcels of energy from the sun. The energy is stored primarily in the form of complex carbohydrates (starch). Packaged along with carbohydrate are the B vitamins, which help release this energy. If you look at Table 1-1 on the next page showing the distribution of calories in different food groups, you will see that between 9 and 17 percent of the calories in grains are from protein. This is similar to the range that is recommended for our overall dietary intake (10 to 15 percent calories from protein) in Table 1-2. In fact, about half (47 percent) of people's protein intake and 51 percent of our calories (energy) come from grains. As shown in the Vegetarian Food Guide, the minimum number of servings recommended for most adults is six. Keep in mind that at many meals, you are likely to eat several servings of grain products, for example, two slices of bread in a sandwich, two or more half-cup servings of steaming pasta, or an extra-big bowl of cereal.

Whole compared with refined grains

The outer layers (bran) and the inner core (germ) of whole grains are concentrated sources of trace minerals: iron, zinc, magnesium, chromium, and many more. When grains are refined, the bran and germ

TABLE I-1

Distribution of calories from protein, fat, and carbohydrate by food group in the Vegetarian Food Guide

% CALORIES FROM:	PROTEIN	FAT	CARBOHYDRATE
GRAINS	9–17	5–16	67–82
VEGETABLES	8–40	1–11	49–91
FRUITS	1–8	1–5	91–94
MILK & ALTERNATIVES:			
Tofu, firm	40	49	11
White, navy, great northern, & black turtle beans	24–27	2–4	69–73
Almonds, sesame butters	11–14	74–76	13
Broccoli, bok choy, kale, napa cabbage	23–36	9–11	53–67
2% milk*	27	35	38
Assorted cheeses	25–39	57–74	1–4
BEANS & ALTERNATIVES:			
Peas, lentils, & most beans	21–30	1–3	67–71
Garbanzo beans (chick-peas)	21	14	65
Silken tofu	44	39	17
Textured soy protein	60	3	37
Nuts & seeds	11–14	74–76	13
Eggs	35	62	3

*This milk is 2 percent fat by weight but more than one-third (35 percent) of its calories come from fat. The carbohydrate present is lactose, the sugar associated with lactose intolerance.

TABLE I-2

Distribution in diet recommended by World Health Organization*

% CALORIES FROM:	PROTEIN	FAT	CARBOHYDRATE
	10–15%	15–30%	55–75%

*World Health Organization Study Group on Diet, Nutrition and Prevention of Non-communicable Diseases. Geneva, Switzerland, Technical Report Series No. 797. 1991.

are removed. In the process, most of the trace minerals, many vitamins, such as folate and vitamin E, and the bulk of the fiber are lost. The recipes in this book focus on whole grains, and use of refined products has been kept to a minimum. Options such as whole wheat, unbleached, or all-purpose flour are suggested so that people in transition may choose whichever they prefer.

In the shift towards a plant-based diet, one adjustment that may help a great deal is to change the concept of what constitutes a meal. In the 20th century, much to the dismay of their coronary arteries, people in North America and Europe became accustomed to meals centered around hefty portions of meat, fish, and poultry. This way of dining has been a fairly recent development in the history of mankind's culinary adventures, and can be viewed as an experiment that is showing poor results. For most of our ancestors, the bulk of calories came from plant foods, a pattern that is still found at the majority of family meals worldwide. Current nutrition recommendations from the World Health Organization and numerous scientific review committees from around the world strongly advocate a return to complex carbohydrates. Rice, pasta, and grain-based meals are reclaiming a central place on the dinner tables of health-conscious Americans.

While the cereal foods have an important part to play as providers of energy, B vitamins, and trace minerals, they are deficient in vitamins A and C, and that leads us to the next important food group.

Vegetable and Fruit Groups:
nature's healers, the protective foods

You probably learned in grade school that oranges, strawberries, and sweet red peppers provide us with vitamin C. The yellow, orange, red, and green foods in the Vegetable and Fruit Groups are also rich in beta-carotene, the brightly colored form of vitamin A in plant foods. Vitamins C and A are antioxidants. Antioxidants protect us from highly reactive chemicals in our bodies (free radicals) that cause destructive changes in nearby molecules, sometimes setting up chain reactions. This process, unchecked, can lead to disease.

Currently there is an explosion of interest among scientists regarding the discovery and identification of a vast array of naturally occurring chemicals in vegetables and fruit that guard us against disease when we consume these foods. Antioxidants, the isoflavones we described earlier in the section on soyfoods, and hundreds of other protective substances in plant foods have been identified and grouped together under the name "phytochemicals," meaning "plant chemicals."

Vegetables and fruits are noted for their absence of fat—avocados and olives are exceptions. Many vegetables and fruits are good sources of folate, a vitamin required to make new cells, for the maintenance of heart health, and of prime importance during pregnancy.

You'll get added health benefits when you eat a vitamin c-rich vegetable or fruit at the same meal with an item from the Beans & Alternatives Group. This is because the vitamin c interacts with the iron from beans or other foods in this group, making the iron two to three times more available for absorption. Vegetables that are particularly helpful, since they provide more than 30 milligrams of vitamin c in a 1/2-cup serving, are broccoli, Brussels sprouts, cabbages, cauliflower, collards, kale, kohlrabi, peppers, and snow peas. Fruits that are excellent sources of vitamin c are cantaloupe, citrus fruits and juices, guava, kiwifruit, papaya, strawberries, and vitamin c-fortified juices. Combinations that help iron absorption are not unusual or difficult to assemble. Sweet and Sour Tofu on page 152 is a good example, and good combinations are likely present in many of your familiar meals. You help your iron absorption whenever you eat a salad along with any bean or tofu dish, particularly when the salad is made with sweet peppers or any of the foods listed above. The combination of fruit and soy milk or tofu in the Fruit Shakes on page 62 has the same effect.

Milk & Alternatives Group: calcium-rich foods

In North America, we tend to think of milk and milk products as *the* calcium foods and as *the* factor responsible for lifelong bone health. Milk is indeed a concentrated source of calcium, yet an intake of 2 or even 4 cups of milk per day for every American clearly isn't the solution to all our problems of osteoporosis. The sedentary lifestyles and high-animal protein, high-salt diets, which lead to excessive calcium loss, are an integral part of the calcium balance equation. Many dietary and lifestyle factors figure in the equation. For strong bones:

Avoid these: a diet that causes calcium loss (too much salt, alcohol, and protein, especially animal protein) and cigarette smoking

Include these: regular weight-bearing exercise, about 15 minutes per day of sunlight exposure on face and hands, and a diet with adequate amounts of nutrients that build bones—vitamins A, C, D, and K, and the minerals magnesium, zinc, boron, and calcium.

America's focus on milk as the only source of dietary calcium is a consequence of food guides based on European eating patterns and of TV advertising and educational materials provided by dairy councils. Foods such as collards, black beans, calcium-fortified tortillas, fortified soy milk, tofu, and Oriental greens are generally ignored as significant sources of calcium. Although these foods are not as concentrated in calcium as milk, they have proven effective for population groups with lifestyles that support bone health. The calcium contributors are listed as Milk & Alternatives in the Vegetarian Food Guide.

National food guides recommend a daily intake of 2 to 3 cups of milk and its products, supplying 600 to 900 milligrams calcium. When we use plant alternatives, it makes sense to work with servings equivalent to a half-cup of milk (since the plant foods tend to be a little less concentrated as calcium sources). Thus the Vegetarian Food Guide has a similar recommendation: 4 to 6 half-cup servings of milk or 4 to 6 servings of the alternatives, supplying approximately 600 to 900 milligrams calcium (6 to 8 servings during pregnancy and lactation and for teens).

The addition of calcium-rich plant foods to the diet is a bonus for just about everyone: vegetarians, meat eaters, those who use some dairy products, and others who use none at all. In this book, we feature these foods in a variety of tasty, easy dishes originating from around the globe.

The nutritional notes found below many recipes indicate those that are reliable calcium sources. Those that provide between 100 and 200 milligrams calcium per serving are rated as a good source of calcium. Those with more than 200 milligrams per serving are described as an excellent source (page 37).

Your day's supply of calcium is absorbed more efficiently when taken in smaller servings over the course of a day, rather than when consumed in large quantities all at once. Thus, eating 4 to 6 servings of calcium-rich foods in meals and snacks is an effective way of maintaining bone density.

Some of the milk alternatives may be new to you. Kale, broccoli (two dark-green members of the cabbage family) and the light-green napa cabbage (also known as Chinese cabbage or sui choy) have risen in popularity in recent years. Once they were the butt of jokes and were served as overcooked and unwelcome parts of dinner, if at all. Now photos of these deep or pale green vegetables grace the food sections of newspapers and magazines. One reason for this change is research proving the exceptionally high availability to the body of the calcium present in these greens. Other valuable features are the presence of health-supportive antioxidants, and phytochemicals that help block the development of cancers.

Tofu can be an excellent calcium source when set with calcium salts. Choose tofu with a calcium salt, such as calcium sulphate or calcium gluconate, on the ingredient list.

Some calcium-rich foods are also concentrated sources of energy: tofu, almonds, and almond butter. Sesame tahini is a little lower in calcium, but contributes creaminess and some calcium to sauces (page 185) and soups (page 113). Calcium-fortified soy milk can be used in rice pudding or as a warm beverage.

On the other hand, some calcium-rich foods are very low in fat: figs, greens, hijiki seaweed, and white or black beans.

Although the specific beans and greens listed above are good sources of calcium, others are not. Kidney beans, for example, are low in calcium. Spinach and chard contain calcium but it is not bioavailable, as the calcium present is locked into a complex with a substance called oxalate or oxalic acid.

Soy- and grain-based beverages that are not fortified with calcium are not part of this food group and should not be relied on as calcium sources.

Note that some foods count as servings in the Milk & Alternatives Group and in another group. For example, greens are also in the Vegetables group; whereas calcium-set tofu and white and black beans are in the next food group that we cover.

Beans & Alternatives Group: for protein, iron, and zinc

Table 1-1 (page 27), which shows the distribution of calories from protein, fat, and carbohydrate in the food groups, illustrates that all of the
groups contribute protein to our diets. Legumes (beans, peas, and
lentils) tend to be a little more concentrated as protein sources than are
many other foods, with 21 to 30 percent of their calories derived from
protein. Note that we need only 10 to 15 percent of our calories to come
from protein (Table 1-2), so this gives us more than enough, and can be
balanced by the lower-protein plant foods. The pattern of amino acids in
legumes, and especially in tofu and many other soy foods, tends to be
well suited to human needs. The abundance and quality of protein in
legumes makes them especially valuable for growing children and for
others with high protein needs. African Stew (page 128) and Crispy Tofu
Fingers (page 132) can quickly become family favorites.

Beans, like all plant foods, are cholesterol free. When we omit meat
from the diet, the initial response of many people is, "Where will you get
your protein?" Since we easily get enough protein, a more fitting ques-
tion would be, "Where will you get your saturated fat and cholesterol?"

The Beans & Alternatives Group is a primary provider of iron. A lack
of this mineral results in fatigue, irritability, and other symptoms of
iron-deficiency anemia. This food group also features zinc, a mineral
with many important roles to play in our immune systems, growth, sex-
ual development and function, and sense of taste. An adequate intake of
zinc is essential at any age, and particularly during pregnancy and during
the growing years from infancy through adolescence.

Omega-3 fatty acid sources

Certain components of oils, known as the omega-6 and omega-3 fatty
acids, are essential to life. They transport substances in and out of cells
and help to regulate body function. These substances are as fundamental
to human life as electricity is to a light bulb. The essential fatty acid
(linoleic acid) in the omega-6 family is fairly easy to come by and is present in such a wide range of plant foods that an insufficiency is unlikely.
Getting enough of the essential omega-3 fatty acid (linolenic acid) isn't
so easy. Furthermore, omega-3 fatty acids are extremely vulnerable to

destruction by heat, light, and oxygen. Because of this, we have made a point of including ingredients high in omega-3 fatty acids in many of the recipes.

The easiest way to get your day's supply of omega-3s is by using flaxseed oil (see page 218), used in salad dressings on pages 105, 109, and 112. Other good sources are unrefined canola and soybean oils, freshly shelled walnuts, and tofu. For best retention of these fragile oils, food sources should be raw or exposed to as little cooking as possible. In the case of tofu, a good choice would be to add tofu to a dish near the end of the cooking time. Ground flaxseed is a source when eaten raw (for example sprinkled on cereal or salad), with 4 teaspoons providing your daily supply of omega-3s. (We do not recommend this source for children, or adults with swallowing problems, as the ground seeds swell up on contact with water.) Much of the oil present in leafy greens is from omega-3 fatty acids, however they contain so little oil that they can't be relied on as your only source.

Vitamin B12

Find a source (food or supplement) supplying 2 micrograms (mcg) of vitamin B12 daily, and 3 micrograms during pregnancy and lactation. To get 2 micrograms for a day's supply, you may choose fortified foods, such as breakfast cereals or meat analogs, which supply over 30 percent of the Daily Value for vitamin B12; check the Nutrition Facts on the label. Alternatively you could use 2 teaspoons of Red Star Vegetarian Support Formula Nutritional Yeast Powder (page 218). Unlike brewer's yeast, which is an industrial by-product, and baker's yeast, which is intended for leavening, Red Star nutritional yeast is grown on a B12-enriched medium and is a tasty ingredient in many of our recipes. For lacto-ovo-vegetarians, 2 micrograms is supplied by 4 large eggs, 4 1/2 cups of milk or yogurt, or 17 ounces of cheese. You may find it easiest to use a vitamin supplement several times a week. On the label, vitamin B12 may also be listed as cobalamin; most supplements supply 25 to 50 micrograms or more and can be cut into quarters.

Vitamin D

We produce our own vitamin D when we have adequate exposure to sunlight (ultraviolet radiation) on our hands and face. It doesn't take a lot of sun to get our daily quota: 10 to 15 minutes of sun for light skinned people, and 1/2 hour or more for dark skinned people. In northern regions, adults generally store enough vitamin D to last them through the winter, whereas young children will need a fortified food or supplement.

Balance in protein, fat, and carbohydrate

In addition to food guides, nutritional guidelines have been developed to assist people in adopting healthful eating patterns. One such guideline gives us an idea of how our calories should be distributed between

TABLE 1-3

Distribution in diet recommended by World Health Organization*

% CALORIES FROM:	PROTEIN	FAT	CARBOHYDRATE
	10–15%	15–30%	55–75%

Distribution of calories from protein, fat, and carbohydrate in selected foods in the standard American diet.

% CALORIES FROM:	PROTEIN	FAT	CARBOHYDRATE
Mayonnaise	1	98	1
Low-calorie mayonnaise	0	79	21
Potato chips	5	59	36
French fries	5	46	49
Regular beef patty, broiled	34	66	0
Lean beef patty, broiled	48	52	0
Chicken thigh, roasted, skinless	51	49	0
Sockeye salmon	53	47	0
Cheddar cheese	25	74	1
Parmesan cheese	37	60	3
Part-skim mozzarella cheese	39	57	4
Grilled cheese sandwich	18	51	31
Sugars	0	0	100
Oils, margarine, and butter	0	100	0

protein, fat, and carbohydrate. Extensive scientific research indicates a connection between overconsumption of dietary fat and chronic diseases common to the affluent countries of the world: coronary artery disease, various cancers, hypertension, strokes, bowel disorders, and diabetes. Thus the Surgeon General has concluded that "overconsumption of certain dietary components is now a major concern for Americans. While many food factors are involved, chief among them is the disproportionate consumption of foods high in fats, often at the expense of foods high in complex carbohydrates and fiber—such as vegetables, fruits and whole grain products—that may be more conducive to health."

The current intake of fat in the United States is 33 to 34 percent of total calories, on average. This being the average, some people are eating a lot more than that! In a 1991 technical report, the World Health Organization recommended that adults receive between 15 and 30 percent of the total calories in their diet from fats (Table 1-2). They added that the upper limit of 30 percent should be considered an interim goal and that health benefits could be realized if fat intake is in the 15 to 20 percent range. Table 1-3, on the previous page, shows the calorie distribution for a few of the foods that contribute to high levels of dietary fat in the American diet. Table 1-1, on page 27, presents calorie distributions of the foods in the Vegetarian Food Guide. As you see, plant foods contain oils without any addition of fat to a recipe. Compare your favorite foods in Tables 1-1 and 1-3 with the distribution of calories among protein, fat, and carbohydrate recommended by the World Health Organization (Table 1-2).

For most Americans, a shift is needed away from excess trans fatty acids, animal fats, and protein and towards more complex carbohydrate and fiber. Fiber, present only in plant foods, does not contribute calories. However, it does play a major role in maintaining bowel health and is a valuable part of the defense against many chronic diseases. As you can see from these tables, current dietary recommendations translate into a diet centered on plant foods.

Different needs

The tables in this chapter are here to help you make dietary choices, depending on your particular needs. As shown in Table 1-4 (page 37), each food group in the Vegetarian Food Guide offers both low-fat and higher-fat selections.

Many people will find, to their delight, that an emphasis on grains, vegetables, fruits, and legumes will cause them to shed unwanted pounds. A focus on low-fat foods is beneficial in the treatment and reversal of coronary artery disease and for weight loss.

Vesanto Melina has had the privilege of working as a staff dietitian with Dr. Dean Ornish's Open Your Heart retreats at the Claremont Hotel in Berkeley. The books *Dr. Ornish's Program for Reversing Heart Disease* and *Eat More, Weigh Less* (see page 231) describe more fully the eating and lifestyle pattern that has proven to be successful in halting and reversing heart disease, and in achieving healthy body weights. This program is now being explored for its usefulness in the treatment of prostate cancer. Moderate amounts of tofu, soy milk, and flaxseed oil have now been added to the original low-fat dietary guidelines, as sources of essential fatty acids.

For those people who wish to follow such a program, turn to the list of recipes that are particularly low in fat (page 56). These recipes fit the guidelines of Dr. Ornish's program; some include soyfoods and flaxseed oil as ingredients (page 218).

Most people benefit by including foods from both the low- and higher-fat columns. The fats present in natural plant foods do not have the disadvantages of the trans fatty acids and excessive saturated fat that are so prevalent in the standard American diet. Plant oils aid in mineral absorption and provide valuable phytochemicals, fat-soluble vitamins, and essential fatty acids.

Adults who are a little leaner than they want to be, athletes who burn calories at a great rate, and active hungry children and teens need some of the higher-fat options from Table 1-4 as a regular part of their diets. The recommendation for 15 to 30 percent calories from fat applies to adults; however, active young children on a healthy plant-based diet thrive on a somewhat higher proportion of fat and the regular inclusion of foods such as tofu and nut butters.

TABLE 1-4

Low-fat and higher-fat choices in each food group

FOOD GROUP	LOW-FAT	HIGH-FAT
GRAINS *Energy Foods*	Grains and pastas are low in fat.	Some grain products are high in fat, such as croissants, most crackers, and muffins
VEGETABLES *Protective Foods*	Almost all vegetables are low fat.	Avocados, olives
FRUITS *Protective Foods*	Fruits and juices	—
BEANS & ALTERNATIVES *Protein, iron &* *zinc foods*	Peas, lentils, most beans, low-fat meat substitutes/analogues, textured soy protein (TVP), low-fat soy milk	Soybeans*, tofu*, regular soy milk*, peanuts, nuts, coconut, seeds, nut & seed butters, eggs
MILK & ALTERNATIVES *Calcium-rich foods*	Broccoli, kale, napa cabbage, bok choy, light tofu set with calcium, seaweed, low-fat calcium-fortified soy & grain milks	Almonds, sesame seeds and their butters, tofu made with calcium*, regular calcium-fortified soy milk*, skim milk, cheeses

*These ingredients and flaxseed oil are included with our low-fat recipes because they provide the essential omega-3 fatty acids. Soyfoods also contain the health-protective isoflavones.

TABLE 1-5

DV (Daily Value) Rating System

NUTRIENT	DV STANDARD	EXCELLENT SOURCE	GOOD SOURCE
Calcium	1 g (1000 mg)	> 200 mg	100–199 mg
Iron	18 mg	> 3.6 mg	1.8–3.5 mg
Magnesium	400 mg	> 80 mg	40–79 mg
Zinc	15 mg	> 3 mg	1.5–2.9 mg
Folate	400 mcg	> 0.08 mg	0.04–.07 mg
Niacin	20 mg	> 4 mg	2–3.9 mg
Riboflavin	1.7 mg	> 0.34 mg	0.17–0.33 mg
Thiamin	1.5 mg	> 0.3 mg	0.15–0.29 mg
Vitamin A	5,000 IU*	> 1,000 IU	500–999 IU
Vitamin B12	6 mcg**	> 1.2 mcg	0.6–1.1 mcg
Vitamin E	30 IU	> 6 IU	3–5.9 IU

*International Units

**Although the recommended intake for B12 for a day is 2 mcg, the DV is set at an earlier, unnecessarily high recommendation of 6 mcg. Thus if a food label indicates that a serving provides 33 percent of the DV, it actually provides the entire 2 mcg for a day's supply.

Healthy, Delicious, and Easy

Note that vegetarian diets with a heavy reliance on grilled cheese sandwiches, full-fat dairy products, and eggs can be high in saturated fat and cholesterol.

Nutritional analysis of recipes

For recipes listing alternative ingredients, for example flaxseed oil or canola oil, analysis was done using the first ingredient listed (in this case flaxseed oil). Where there is a range, such as 1 to 2 tablespoons, the lesser quantity is used. Unless otherwise specified, optional ingredients are not included in the analysis. Nutrient values greater than 1 have been rounded to the nearest whole number.

The nutritional analysis for each recipe compares the quantities of selected vitamins and minerals in one serving with a standard used in food labeling known as the Daily Value (DV), shown in Table 1-5. Where a serving provides more than 20 percent of the DV for a particular nutrient, it is listed as an excellent source of that nutrient. Where a serving provides 10 to 19 percent of the DV, it is listed as a good source.

The nutrient analysis shows, in alphabetical order, the minerals calcium, iron, magnesium, potassium, and zinc, and the vitamins folate, niacin, riboflavin, thiamin, and vitamins A, B_6, B_{12}, C, and E, wherever these are present in significant amounts.

Fiber and sodium

The amounts of fiber and sodium provided by each serving of a recipe are listed in grams (g) and milligrams (mg) respectively. These can be compared with the recommended intakes of 20 to 40 grams of fiber and of up to 2,400 milligrams of sodium per day.

Grams and calories from protein, fat, and carbohydrate

The grams of protein, fat, and carbohydrate provided by each serving of a recipe are also shown. In addition, the percentage of calories from each of these three nutrients is shown and can be compared with the recommendation for overall caloric distribution summarized in Table 1-2.

Because fat is a much more concentrated energy source (9 calories per gram) than are protein and carbohydrate (4 calories per gram), a tablespoon of oil (14 grams) added to a recipe may add only a few grams of fat to each serving, but markedly increase the percentage of calories from fat.

The DV's do not provide a standard for intake of omega-3 fatty acids. Canada and Britain have specific guidelines for intake of these essential components of oils. The Canadian Nutrition Recommendations suggest that omega-3 fatty acids provide 0.5 percent of the total caloric intake. On the basis of a 2,000 calorie diet, that would be 10 calories or 1.1 grams. (If a pure omega-3 oil existed in nature, this would be equivalent to 1/4 teaspoon.) The form of omega-3s found in plant oils is essential and we have the ability to convert it to the form found in fish oils. The different forms have various regulatory functions in the body. The efficiency of our conversion is a matter of debate. Some health experts suggest that when all omega-3s are from plant sources and none are from fish oils, the recommended amount should be doubled; other scientists advocate even higher amounts. We have used 2.2 milligrams of omega-3 fatty acids daily as a guideline. Since 57 percent of flaxseed oil comes from omega-3s, 1 teaspoon of flaxseed oil gives a day's supply.

This chapter provides a concise summary of the nutritional information that will help you build and maintain optimal health with a plant-based diet. The Vegetarian Food Guide is meant to be a reference standard for use when averaging intake over a few days, rather than a rigid rule for planning each day's menus. It illustrates the number of servings that give a balance of nutrients from every food group. It suggests minimum and maximum intake for adults of differing sizes and activity levels. If you record your intake for a few days and compare it with the Guide, you'll get an idea of the strengths and weaknesses of your current pattern.

With an awareness of the ingredients you'd like to emphasize in your meals, you can create nutritious new dishes that you and your family will thoroughly enjoy. Chapter 2 offers guidance from chef Joseph Forest, who loves working with food and is truly gifted in the kitchen. It is presented so that your experience with the recipes brings you the utmost joy and well-being.

VESANTO MELINA

References for Nutrient Analysis

The Food Processor, Quality Nutrition Analysis Software and Databases, ESHA Research, 1997. 1-800-659-3742 (Nutritional analysis program used for recipe analyses)

United States Department of Agriculture, Agriculture Research Service. Agricultural Handbook No. 8. This is available at university libraries and on the internet at http://www.nal.usda.gov/fnic/foodcomp/

For Weight Watchers members…

The dietary fiber grams, calories, and fat grams are listed for each recipe to calculate the points per serving.

Chapter Two

Notes from Chef Joseph

Drawing together individual food items to create a recipe is similar to a conductor bringing the sound of individual instruments together to create a symphony. The results can be spectacular and the rewards enduring. You are the conductor of your own kitchen symphony.

Food as passion

Food is the great passion of my life. As far back as I can remember, all of my senses have been curious about the endless nuances surrounding food. Food is my doorway into the world of alchemy: colors brighten, textures soften, and shapes emerge and disappear before my eyes and in my hands as I marry one food to another. Under the influence and purposeful direction of fire, air, and water, earth is transformed from humble origins into celebrated goodness. This process not only nourishes my life—it is my life.

Not everyone has this kind of relationship with food. There are some who believe that eating is a chore, an interruption from a more important task. Others consider themselves inept in the kitchen and consequently fling the most basic ingredients together meal after meal. For still others, preparing meals can be a daunting experience resulting in chaos. These situations can lead to nutritionally inadequate eating patterns.

This chapter was written to help you integrate the elements that precede and include food preparation. One of these elements is the nutritional balance between food groups in your eating pattern, as outlined in Chapter 1. Choice of good quality ingredients is another important component, as are strong organizational skills in the kitchen, including the preparation, cooking, and presentation of food. Consider all these components as ingredients in a recipe for health. Time and attention given to these elements and how they are assembled under your direction will have a significant impact on the quality of your life.

A central theme in the orchestration of cooking is choice; numerous choices present themselves every day. What shall I eat tonight? Are higher-quality items worth the extra expense? What method of cooking should I use? How much time do I have to cook? These are choices that need to be made according to your schedule, tastes, and preferences, and they will be addressed here in the hope that cooking will become and continue to be a source of enjoyment.

These recipes have been created with health in mind, yet we all know that unless flavor is present it doesn't matter how healthy food is. Our approach is to use foods, herbs, and spices that are fresh and in as natural a state as possible to create great-tasting food. Furthermore, we encourage you to use each recipe as a guideline, to work with it according to the ingredients you have on hand, adjusting it to your own particular tastes.

A distinct feature in many of these recipes is oil-free sautéing for those who wish to reduce the amount of oil in their diet. This cooking technique is straightforward and does not require any extra time. Those who believe that the use of oil is critical to cooking may want to try the oil-free option on occasion to see if this method has merit.

Choices in the marketplace

The market is brimming with variety. Food stores offer every conceivable product in myriad shapes, sizes, and colors. Produce departments feature fruits and vegetables from every part of the world. Trade names and food brands compete for your attention and loyalty at each turn. All these possibilities add up to a mountain of decisions and can be confusing. Knowledge of our Vegetarian Food Guide, coupled with discernment, are useful tools in navigating through this land of a thousand choices. To help narrow down your decisions, consider these two recommended food categories:

1. Those that retain their natural complement of nutrients
2. Those that are organically grown

Foods that retain their natural complement of nutrients

Nature packages food in perfect ways that we have yet to improve upon. Plants offer energy in the form of complex carbohydrates, building properties via protein, and essential fatty acids in oils, combined in amounts that are exquisitely balanced. When foods are whole, or close to their natural states, elements such as vitamins and phytochemicals provide natural defenses against deterioration. For example, when a walnut is in its shell, protective membranes surround the meat of the nut, and vitamin E and other antioxidants in the nut oils protect valuable omega-3 fatty acids from oxidation and rancidity. After months on a store shelf, shelled walnuts have lost much of their flavor along with the health-supportive properties they are capable of imparting to us. For a fresh product, shell nuts just before use or choose shelled nuts from a store that keeps them in the refrigerator or has a high turnover of product.

Foods such as fruits, vegetables, unrefined cereal grains, legumes, nuts, and seeds can be found in the marketplace with little change from their state in the farmer's field. Such foods have high nutritional density, that is, they provide plenty of nutritional value per calorie of food energy. They are also richer in natural flavors, and do not need artificial flavor enhancers. It makes sense to center your diet on these foods.

Do you imagine that the choice of eating healthy requires that you spend long hours in the kitchen preparing foods from scratch? With the growing appetite for healthy foods, more ingredients are available that have been processed to make them easy to use, at the same time retaining top nutritional quality. Examples are nut and seed butters, whole grain pastas, and soy foods, which include tofu. Our recipes are full of such ingredients. Spend a little time browsing the aisles or freezer of a local health food store or natural foods section of a major supermarket. You'll discover many new nutrition-packed products. Many of these products didn't exist even a few years ago, and the flavor and quality have come a long way in our competitive marketplace. Another area of growth is convenience foods. Deli counters offer a wonderful array of prepared foods. Consider buying one or two tasty side dishes at a deli to accompany a quickly prepared salad and cooked grain at home.

Organic foods

Concerns about the effects of pesticides and herbicides have led to organic farming methods that don't damage the world's soil, fresh water supply, and atmosphere. Organic agriculture is a system of management that uses safer and environmentally friendlier methods for growing food. They include natural pest control, crop rotation, composting, mulching, and the use of pest-resistant seed varieties, along with the avoidance of any irradiation or genetic engineering. The purposes are to produce food with the fewest possible toxins and to create a fertile environment for plants as well as birds, predatory insects, earthworms, and microorganisms. The result is health-supporting food and richer and more arable soil. Consider that every time you buy organic, you are making a powerful vote for a healthier world to live in.

The transition to organic

Choosing to put organic food on your table can be as important a change as opting for a vegetarian diet. In both cases the change can be made gradually: you don't have to convert your refrigerator or your pantry overnight. As you become familiar with organic foods, you'll find they are becoming more readily available. Produce departments of large food stores are beginning to offer a variety of organic food products, as managers discover positive customer response. Farmers' markets, natural food stores, and co-ops carry a wide selection of local organic produce.

Choose the best quality ingredients your budget allows

Since nutrients are a big factor in supporting health, it makes sense to purchase ingredients that give you the biggest nutritional return for your dollar. The cost of outfitting your kitchen with healthy food might appear expensive, yet the cost often proves worthwhile in the long run. Perhaps you can learn from one of my experiences. When I used to purchase pure olive oil for use in hummus, I would use 1/4 cup of oil to satisfy my taste. Since I have discovered extra-virgin olive oil, I've reduced the amount of oil I use to 1 tablespoon due to the distinctive flavor of the oil. (Olives are pressed several times to extract every possible drop of oil. The first pressings, which are the most flavorful, are referred to as "extra virgin-olive oil." The last pressings, labeled "pure olive oil" are not as flavorful.) At first the oil appears to cost more; however, I get better mileage from the higher-quality oil, since I use less.

You too will become familiar with new ingredients and consequently will be in a better position to make decisions. When shopping, ask questions about the products you examine, and read labels. Make a choice, and if it's not the best one for you, make another choice. In time you will become more confident in the use of a variety of new kitchen staples.

Organization is the key to your success

Once you have gathered an assortment of good ingredients, the next step is preparing them. This is where the system breaks down for many people. The manner in which you approach your food preparation can make or break your cooking enjoyment. The key to success is organization.

During my chef's training, the emphasis was on advance preparation to buffer the pressures and unexpected requests that bombard a professional kitchen during peak service times. A lot of time was devoted to this advance organization. The French term for this process is *mis en place,* meaning "everything in its place." We developed this skill so that minimal time was spent running around the kitchen once service began.

Like a busy professional chef, you have deadlines, pressures, unexpected interruptions, and last minute requests in your own life. You may not have as much time to spend in the kitchen as you would like; however, some rudimentary organizational skills can maximize your productivity and efficiency. The following steps can help you have a more enjoyable experience in the kitchen.

1. Read your recipe first

Develop the habit of reading your chosen recipes from beginning to end. This gives you an overview of the foods, techniques, cooking times, and equipment required. It also stimulates your thinking about the task at hand and how you are going to accomplish it.

2. Gather all equipment needed

This includes cutting board, knives, mixing bowls, measuring cups, spoons, food processor, and pots. This step may prompt you to read the recipe again, which is the real key to the exercise. Reading the recipe a second time deepens your understanding of what you are about to perform. The clearer your idea of what you are about to do, the less chaos there will be at the kitchen counter or stovetop.

3. Gather all the ingredients

Knowing up front that you have all the ingredients eliminates the frustration of discovering halfway through a recipe that you didn't replenish an important staple on your last shopping trip. This step also saves time. Gathering everything at the beginning requires less time than if you periodically interrupt your cutting or measuring to return to the refrigerator or cupboard for an additional ingredient. This step also allows you to be more present once you have begun your preparation.

While you are preparing ingredients for the recipe, this is the time to preheat the oven, boil water for pasta, or prewarm the skillet or soup pot at the lowest setting.

4. Set up your counter space

This is not so much a step as a pattern to follow each time you prepare food. How you arrange and organize your ingredients and equipment determines how smoothly the final product comes into being. My approach to how I prepare the Szechuan Vegetables over Buckwheat Noodles, page 153, might serve as an example.

All my kitchen utensils are already assembled in a wicker basket to the left of the stove. I lay a flat, damp dishcloth on the counter and set my cutting board on top to prevent slipping—a valuable safety tip when using sharp knives. My skillet is preheating on the lowest heat setting. I gather all ingredients to the left of the cutting board and wash those that require it. As vegetables are cut they are placed in separate piles on a baking sheet or large plate to the right of the board. All herbs and spices are measured into a small bowl, wet ingredients into a second bowl. Ingredients no longer needed are returned to the cupboard or refrigerator. I now proceed to the stove where I am poised to cook.

How you set up your counter space is partly determined by how much space you have to work with. If you are short of counter space, perhaps a portable table such as a TV tray could be brought into the kitchen when needed, to help in organizing your ingredients.

When all ingredients are prepped and gathered within arm's reach, the actual cooking becomes a much easier task, whether you are stir-frying or assembling sushi. You won't have to worry about burning the onions while you're still cutting carrots. Your counter space will be much clearer, thus your kitchen won't look as if Hurricane Andrew just passed through. Developing this habit can go a long way toward alleviating kitchen chaos.

The use of oil in cooking

Overall, consumption of oil is high in our national diet, but this is changing as the evidence builds linking high fat and oil intake to a decline in health. Many people believe that oil is crucial to cooking and that without its liberal use, cooking is not possible. Vegetable oil in cooking and baking does serve several purposes.

- ◆ Perhaps the most obvious one is that it prevents food from sticking to the skillet, pot, or grill.
- ◆ Oil is an excellent conductor of heat, so when foods are coated with oil at high temperatures, as in a stir-fry, they cook very rapidly.
- ◆ Vegetable oil and fat add moisture to food and consequently increase the shelf life or quality of products like bread, cakes, and cookies.
- ◆ Adding oil to food gives it smoothness and a pleasant "mouth feel," as it does with hummus.
- ◆ Perhaps the most common feature of oil is its ability to act as a carrier for flavor, as evident in salad dressings.

No-oil cooking as an option

The limited quantities of oils found in nature contain certain components that are an essential part of good nutrition. On the other hand, hydrogenated fats, such as shortenings, are high in trans fatty acids. Many North Americans consume too much fat because of widespread use of frying. Realizing this, a growing number of people with health and weight problems are cutting back on their use of added fats and oils.

Those looking for ways to reduce the calories from fat in their diet have found that, instead of sautéing food in oil, they can sauté with vegetable stock or water. Many of the recipes in this book feature this liquid sautéing method, however recipes also provide oil as an option. The analyses below these recipes include nutrient figures for both methods. You may want to compare the distribution of calories without oil, with oil, and with the recommended caloric distribution in Table 1-2 on page 27. You may want to use the oil-free cooking method exclusively, on occasion, or not at all.

Whether you use vegetable stock, water, or oil for sautéing food, the goal is the same: to develop flavor and bring out the sweetness of the vegetables. As the sautéing liquid evaporates, the sugars in the vegetables caramelize and add sweetness. Sautéing in too much liquid results in boiling, which does not provide the sweetness of caramelization.

The technique for oil-free sautéing is as follows. Sauté vegetables over medium-high heat in 2 tablespoons of vegetable stock or water to start, adding 1 or 2 tablespoons more liquid if necessary. To control the rate of evaporation and to keep it to a minimum, lower the cooking temperature or use a lid. Use stock whenever possible as this adds more flavor than water. A number of vegetable stock powders, canned stocks, and cubes are available on the market, but our recommendation is to avoid products that contain hydrogenated oil. If you want to control the final taste, try making your own stock (page 125). Once you familiarize yourself with this cooking method, keeping a jar of stock on hand in the refrigerator makes sense. You may want to double or triple the recipe and freeze it for up to 3 months. Ice cube trays will hold 2 tablespoons of liquid per cube, which is the amount of liquid that will be called for in most recipes. Once the cubes are frozen, remove them from the tray and store them in a freezer bag as keeping them exposed in the tray for long periods causes them to shrink due to evaporation. Make more, so you always have stock cubes on hand.

Unrefined oils for flavor

If one of the functions of oil is to provide flavor, does reducing oil in the diet mean less flavorful food? The answer is no. The cooking oils that we suggest you eliminate or reduce in the diet are highly-refined commercial oils. Modern oil production subjects seeds and their oils to many processes including hexane solvent extraction, degumming, bleaching, and deodorizing. These processes require temperature ranges of 130° to over 500° for periods of 30 to 60 minutes at a time. The resulting oil is devoid of the nutritional qualities that were originally present in the seed. The oils recommended for use in this book are unrefined, such as those sold by Omega Nutrition USA, Inc. (page 229). Although they too have been crushed, pressing temperatures, particularly for flaxseed oil, range between 86 and 92°. Oils pressed at lower temperatures retain important nutritional elements. Also, these oils carry the flavor of the seed or nut from which they were pressed. For example, extra-virgin olive oil tastes like olives, and unrefined sunflower oil tastes like sunflower seeds. Unrefined oils can be used in salad dressings; sprinkled over rice, noodles, and steamed vegetables; or as a garnish for soup. Flaxseed oil may even be used on Oatmeal Porridge (page 68) or in the Fruit Shake (page 62).

Aromatic oils in herbs and spices for developing flavor

An herb is an aromatic plant used for seasoning food or for medicinal purposes. Culinary herbs such as bay, basil, oregano, parsley, sage, and thyme are mostly grown in temperate climates, and their leaves are the part of the plant used in cooking. Spices, on the other hand, are aromatic plants that are generally pungent and originate from tropical lands. The plant parts generally used are roots (ginger), bark (cinnamon), flowers (saffron), berries (allspice and pepper), seeds (cumin and caraway), pods (vanilla and cardamom), and fruit (anise seed and tamarind).

Herbs and spices draw upon the characteristic aromatic oils contained in the plant. These oils have distinctive aromas, ranging from subtle to intense and when released into food they impart specific tastes and fragrances. In addition, these oils offer distinctive health-supportive properties. For instance, cumin, fennel, and ginger promote digestion. When consistently used in your diet, they can be advantageous to your health.

Scientific investigation has revealed powerful disease preventive roles for phytochemicals found in herbs and spices. For example, the pigment that gives turmeric and curries their distinctive yellow color is curcumin, which also acts to block the development of tumors. Anticancer agents have been identified in dill and caraway. Two components (carnosol and carnosic acid) in rosemary are antioxidants, protective against damaging oxidation reactions. Onions and garlic provide a host of phytochemicals that are effective against development of cancers, blood clotting, and high blood lipids.

Since aromatic oils are very volatile, they begin to disperse into the atmosphere immediately upon harvesting. Consequently, fresh herbs are better to use than dried. The roots, barks, whole seeds, and berries of spices are hardier and will retain their oils longer than the delicate leaves of herbs. However, once ground into powder, they too quickly lose their potency.

Herbs and spices are best purchased from a store where there is a high turnover of these staples. Amber glass jars or opaque containers are a good investment to keep damaging light out. Tight-fitting lids keep the precious aromatic oils in. Avoid storing your herbs and spices near the warm environment of an oven as heat quickly dissipates the valuable oils, making them less effective. Dried herbs should be replaced within six months, spices within one year.

The use of fresh herbs such as basil, thyme, and oregano are recommended over dried, particularly in the summertime when they are more economical and abundant due to kitchen sill and balcony gardening. A conversion ratio for determining the equivalent of fresh herbs to dry is 1 tablespoon of fresh herb equals 1 teaspoon dried herb.

Adjust the seasoning

The last instruction in most recipes, whether written or assumed is "Adjust the seasoning" or "Season to taste." Although this usually implies adding salt and pepper, it is an opportunity to adjust the recipe to suit your tastes and preferences with seasonings or flavorings such as extra garlic, lemon juice, cilantro, etc. The ability to evaluate and correct the final flavors of a dish is a valuable skill, so take the time to be mindful at this stage. Trust your intuition and your taste.

Using the recipe as a guideline

Remember, a recipe is a set of instructions that brings together a set of ingredients to achieve a final product. But these ingredients and instructions are not carved in stone. They are meant to act as a guide to steer you in a particular direction. We encourage you to follow a recipe once to get a sense of it, then decide if it is worth keeping. You may even want to adjust an ingredient or two before you start: for instance, tahini may not be your favorite butter but perhaps almond butter is. Therefore in the Good Morning Granola on page 67, you could exchange one butter for the other. The concentrated apple juice in the same recipe could replace the maple syrup altogether. In soups, a different combination of vegetables or beans may be more to your taste, or maybe you would prefer rice instead of noodles. We do recommend, however, that if you try an ingredient such as tofu or flaxseed oil for the first time, and the recipe isn't pleasing, consider giving the ingredient another chance in a different recipe.

Garnishing as the final adjustment

Before serving, take a few minutes to create an ambiance for the delicious food you have invested time and energy preparing. Garnishing food creates balance, harmony, and beauty. A garnish has a way of uplifting the mood and spirit of the cook as well as those served. On a deeper level, adding a final touch to the meal can be a tremendous act of respect and love, for you, your family, and the food. Simply stated, garnishing is an art form that has the power to nourish the soul.

Garnishes do not have to be as complicated as carving flowers out of carrots or forming a rose bud from the long unbroken peeled skin of a tomato. A garnish should contrast with the main colors of the food and be applied in odd numbers. For example, if olives are the garnish of choice on top of a salad or platter, use 1, 3, or 5 rather than 2, 4, or 6.

Ideas for garnishing your food include chopped or whole leaves of fresh herbs, wedges of lemon or tomato, or capers. Finely diced red, yellow, or orange bell peppers; finely chopped green onion; sprouts; and grated radish, carrot, or zucchini all have their place in adding a final touch to the meal. When sprinkling powders such as paprika over potato salad, place a bit in the palm of one hand and use the other to pinch and sprinkle. There are books that specialize in garnishes, some simple, some very complex. Be inspired to explore this very creative and artistic side of food presentation.

In the past few years, the use of whole flowers or their petals in salads or on the rim of a plate has become an effective way of bringing excitement and raising the enjoyment level of a meal. The delicate reds, blues, purples, and pinks are very pleasing to the eye and can create a new dimension to an eating experience. Be cautious when picking your own flowers by making certain they are edible and haven't been sprayed.

Nourishing properties of beauty

The beauty reflected in the garnish of your plate can be extended to your table. In my own home I arrange fresh cut flowers in a vase and light candles. Eating is a time when I open up to receive more than just nourishment from food. Good company, conversation, music, laughter, and the beauty found at home are nourishing components to my meal that are just as significant as the food I have chosen for its wholesome content. Mirth and joy garnish my table as much as the flowers do. Above all, mealtimes are a time of rest, a place where I truly find comfort in the gifts of Earth.

May your body, mind, and soul be truly nourished through the wise use of food.

JOSEPH FOREST

Chapter Three

Menu Selections

The combination of recipes found in the following menu selections reflect a blending of ingredients, flavors, seasonings, and colors that are common in many homes around the world. Choose a few for a simple meal, or more for a larger gathering or an evening of entertaining. The selections range from the everyday fast and easy dishes found in the American Menu Selections to more complex choices for festive times from the Thanksgiving and Christmas Menu Selections.

American Menu Selections

Chinese Menu Selections

French Menu Selections
Roasted Garlic and Yam Spread with
  Whole Wheat Baguette 82
Split Pea Soup with Veggie Back
  Bacon 123
Deep Green Leafy Salad 94
Flaxseed Oil-Tomato-Basil
  Dressing 105
Mushroom-Lentil Patties with Tomato
  Sauce 144
Dijon Scalloped Potatoes 170
Greens with Tomatoes and Garlic 172
Chocolate Cream Couscous Cake 207

Indian Menu Selections
Papadums
Mulligatawny Soup 120
Basmati Rice Salad 89
Curried Vegetables with Tofu 133
Cauliflower and Yam 167
Potato Subji 177
Tamarind Date Sauce 191
Spinach with Garam Masala 182
Fresh Fruit Salad with Mint 66

Italian Menu Selections
Pesto-the-Best-Oh! on Crusty Rolls 80
Minestrone Soup 118
Caesar Salad 90
Cashew Cheese Lasagna 129
  or Lasagna Al Forno 141
Baked Eggplant 164
Zucchini, Onion, and Tomato 184
Lem-Un-Cheesecake 212

Japanese Menu Selections
Sushi with Pickled Ginger and
  Wasabi 150
Miso Ginger Soup 116
Watercress, Avocado, and Grapefruit
  Salad 101
Teriyaki Tofu 155
Rice 223

Spinach with Gomasio 183
Carrots and Broccoli with Hijiki 166
Apple Kanten 198

Mexican Menu Selections
Avocado Dip with Crackers 72
Quinoa Salad with Lime Dressing 98
Savory Black Bean Stew 147
Mexican Rice 176
Corn with Red Peppers 168
Blueberry Corn Muffins 202

Middle Eastern Menu Selections
Morocc-Un-Butter 79
Spicy Eggplant Soup 122
Pickled Beet and Kale Salad 96
Zucchini Stuffed with Lentils and
  Bulgur 159
Vegetable Kabobs 157
Currant and Cumin Pilaf 169
Figgy Pudding 209

Thanksgiving and Christmas Menu Selections
Festive Holiday Punch 61
Carrot and Yam Soup 115
Apple Walnut Salad 88
Orange Mint Dressing 107
Stuffed Winter Squash 148
Rosemary Gravy or Light Mushroom
  Gravy 189
Cranberry-Ginger Relish 187
Kale and Red Pepper Holly Ring 173
Red Cabbage with Walnuts 178
Blueberry Mince Tarts with Holiday
  Topping 203

Chapter Four

Low-Fat Recipes
for Heart Health or Weight Loss

The recipes in the list that starts on the next page are very low in fat. Those in the list on page 58 play a significant role in low-fat diets, because they supply the essential fatty acids that are absolutely necessary for good health, particularly the omega-3 fatty acid known as linolenic acid. Flaxseed oil is highest in omega-3s; tofu and soy milk have less omega-3s but they do have protective isoflavones. Taken in moderate amounts, these essential fatty acids from plant oils assist with heart health and help one stay on a low-fat regimen. The recipes below follow the guidelines of Dr. Dean Ornish's *Program for Reversing Heart Disease* (listed in the reference section, page 231), plus the later modifications of this program, which include flaxseed oil, tofu, and soy milk. These recipes also fit dietary guidelines for his prostate study.

In recipes where oil (other than flaxseed oil) is listed as an ingredient, omit the oil. Many of these recipes feature a no-oil option cooking technique for sautéeing foods. This method is described in full on page 47 of Chapter 2.

People requiring low sodium intake should omit tamari, salt, and miso. Also, check the ingredient listing on canned goods for salt content.

Low-Fat Recipes in This Book

PAGE	RECIPE NAME	% CALORIES FROM FAT	GRAMS FAT PER SERVING
BEVERAGES			
61	Festive Holiday Punch	2%	0.2 g
62	Fruit Shakes	9%	2.0 g
63	Hot Cran-Apple Cider	2%	0.3 g
BREAKFAST			
65	Fresh Fruit Salad	4%	1 g
67	Happy Heart Muesli (3/4 cup)	9%	3 g
68	Oatmeal Porridge	12%	3 g
DIPS/SPREADS/SNACKS			
73	Black Bean Hummus	3%	0.5 g
78	Hummus (see Variation)	14%	2 g
81	Raw Vegetable Platter	—	—
82	Roasted Garlic and Yam Spread	1%	0.2 g
SALADS			
88	Apple Walnut Salad (without walnuts)	7%	0.4 g
91	Calcium-Rich Greens	9%	0.6 g
92	Couscous Salad (without tahini)	2%	0.4 g
93	David's Garden of Plenty Salad	7%	0.4 g
94	Deep Green Leafy Salad	10%	0.8 g
96	Pickled Beet and Kale Salad	7%	0.6 g
97	Potato Dill Salad with Tofu Mayo	6%	0.8 g
98	Quinoa Salad with Lime Dressing (without oils)	13%	2.7 g
SALAD DRESSINGS			
107	Orange Mint Dressing	1%	0.1 g
108	Oriental Dressing (without oils)	0%	0 g
SOUPS			
114	Black Bean Soup	3%	1 g
115	Carrot and Yam Soup	3%	1 g
117	Lentil Soup	4%	1 g
118	Minestrone Soup	8%	1g
120	Mulligatawny Soup	5%	0.7 g
121	Mushroom Broth	12%	0.4 g
122	Spicy Eggplant Soup	4%	0.5 g
123	Split Pea Soup with Veggie Back Bacon	3%	1 g
124	Vegetable Noodle Soup	4%	0.5g
125	Vegetable Stock	—	—

PAGE	RECIPE NAME	% CALORIES FROM FAT	GRAMS FAT PER SERVING
ENTRÉES			
131	Chili with Textured Soy Protein	5%	2 g
135	Curry in a Hurry	9%	2 g
136	Delicious Sandwiches, Vegetarian Style, low-fat list	—	—
138	Figs and Beans (with stock instead of oil)	4%	1 g
140	Japanese Roll-Up (with tofu mayo)	6%	2 g
145	Mushroom Risotto	7%	3 g
147	Savory Black Bean Stew	4%	1 g
149	Stuffed Winter Squash (without seeds)	10%	4 g
150	Sushi (with tofu instead of avocado, without gomasio)	5%	2 g
154	Ten Tasty Ways to Stuff Your Pita Pockets, low-fat list	—	—
159	Zucchini Stuffed with Lentils and Bulgur	3%	0.6 g
VEGGIES/SIDE DISHES			
162	Baked Potato, low-calorie toppings	—	—
164	Baked Eggplant (without oil)	10%	0.8 g
166	Carrots and Broccoli with Hijiki (without sesame oil)	5%	0.5 g
168	Corn with Red Peppers	1%	0.6 g
169	Currant and Cumin Pilaf	6%	3 g
171	Green Beans with Black Beans	10%	0.7 g
172	Greens with Tomatoes and Garlic	10%	0.7 g
173	Kale and Red Pepper Holly Ring	10%	1 g
175	Mashed Potatoes (with soy milk)	4%	0.6 g
176	Mexican Rice	8%	2 g
180	Seasoned Potato Wedges (baked without oil)	5%	1 g
181	Spaghetti Squash	8%	0.3 g
184	Zucchini, Onion, and Tomato	8%	1 g
SAUCES			
186	Blueberry Orange Sauce	3%	0.4 g
187	Cranberry Ginger Relish	1%	0.1 g
188	Light Mushroom Gravy	5%	0.1 g
191	Tamarind Date Sauce	2%	0.1 g
192	Teriyaki Sauce	0%	0 g
194	Tomato Sauce with Aduki Beans	2%	0.6 g
195	Tomato Sauce with Textured Soy Protein	4%	0.6 g

Recipes High in Essential Fatty Acids: With Tofu, Soy Milk or Flaxseed Oil as Ingredients

Beverages
and Breakfasts

Almond Milk

 For a concentrated source of energy, along with vitamin E, magnesium, and some calcium (88 milligrams per cup) use this nut milk as a beverage, on cereal, or in a fruit shake. Blanched almonds give a whiter, smoother milk. Since some of the trace minerals and fiber are in the pulp, if you strain it, you might want to add the pulp to baking, cereals, soups, gravy, sauces, or rice. For maximum shelf life, store nuts in closed jars or plastic bags in your freezer or refrigerator.

2 cups water

1/2 cup shelled blanched or
   unblanched almonds

1 tablespoon maple syrup or
   other sweetener (optional)

Put water, almonds, and maple syrup (if using) into blender and process on high speed for 1 minute or until smooth. Can be stored in refrigerator for 4 to 5 days. Shake before using.

Makes 2 1/4 cups with pulp.

PER CUP: calories 189, protein: 7g, carbohydrate: 6 g, fat: 16 g, dietary fiber: 4 g, sodium: 6 mg

EXCELLENT SOURCE OF: magnesium, vitamin E
GOOD SOURCE OF: niacin, riboflavin

% CALORIES FROM: protein 14%, fat 74%, carbohydrate 12%

Festive Holiday Punch

Fresh gingerroot makes a rich contribution to this punch and adds a tiny nip for the tongue. Simmering the ginger briefly in water releases its flavor, which is then incorporated with the sweetness of the fruit juices.

1 1/2 cups water

1 cup Sucanat (page 219)
  or brown sugar

3 tablespoons peeled, chopped
  gingerroot

4 whole cloves

1/2 teaspoon ground cinnamon

1/4 teaspoon ground nutmeg

3 cups orange juice

3 cups apple juice

3 cups cranberry juice

1 orange, sliced thinly

In covered pot, bring to boil water, Sucanat, gingerroot, cloves, cinnamon, and nutmeg. Reduce heat, cover, and simmer 5 minutes. Let steep 1 hour. Combine orange, apple, and cranberry juices in large jar or container. Strain ginger concentrate into fruit juices; cover and refrigerate 4 hours. Adjust sweetness. Pour into punch bowl and garnish with orange slices.

Makes 12 servings, each 1 cup

PER 1-CUP SERVING: calories 113, protein: 0.6 g, carbohydrate: 28 g, fat: 0.2 g, dietary fiber: 0.6 g, sodium: 10 mg

EXCELLENT SOURCE OF: vitamin C

% CALORIES FROM: protein 2%, fat 2%, carbohydrate 96%

Fruit Shakes

 These shakes are favorites as quick breakfasts, after-school snacks, boosts for athletes, and nutritious beverages for seniors, especially when made with soy milk that is fortified with calcium and vitamins B_{12} and D. Ripe bananas give the sweetest flavor. You may also replace the fruits used below with seasonal fruits.

Strawberry Shake

1 1/2 cups fresh or frozen strawberries

1 ripe banana

2 cups soy milk or 1 package soft tofu and 3/4 cup water

Place strawberries, banana, and soy milk, or tofu and water in blender or food processor and blend until smooth.

Orange Shake

1 cup frozen orange juice concentrate

1 ripe banana

2 cups soy milk and 1 cup water or 1 package soft tofu and 1 1/2 cups water

Place juice concentrate, banana, and soy milk and water, or tofu and water in blender or food processor and blend until smooth.

Makes 4 servings, each approximately 1 cup

PER SERVING ORANGE SHAKE: calories 177, protein: 5 g, carbohydrate: 37 g, fat: 2 g, dietary fiber: 1 g, sodium: 91 mg

EXCELLENT SOURCE OF: potassium, folate, vitamins C and D
GOOD SOURCE OF: calcium, magnesium, thiamin, riboflavin, vitamin B_{12}

% CALORIES FROM: protein 10%, fat 9%, carbohydrate 81%

Orange Shake analyzed using fortified ProSoya So Nice original soy beverage. Nutrient data will vary with other brands.

Happy Heart Muesli

 You'll look forward to breakfast with this make-ahead combination waiting for you. Prepared the night before, it makes a nourishing instant breakfast for one hungry person, or can be divided between two. Many people like to eat this for dessert or as an evening snack. If you prefer it less sweet, use a combination of apple juice and water. For variations, add grated apple or mashed ripe banana just before serving.

1 1/4 cups apple juice

1 cup rolled oats

2 tablespoons raisins or currants, or chopped dates or nuts

1/8 teaspoon ground cinnamon

Pinch of any 2: ground nutmeg, cardamom, allspice, or cloves

In bowl, combine apple juice, rolled oats, raisins, cinnamon, and the two spices of your choice. Mix, cover, and refrigerate 2 hours or overnight.

Makes 1 large 1 1/2 cup serving or 2 regular servings

PER 3/4 CUP: calories 256, protein: 7 g, carbohydrate: 53 g, fat: 3 g, dietary fiber: 5 g, sodium: 7 mg

EXCELLENT SOURCE OF: thiamin
GOOD SOURCE OF: iron, magnesium, potassium, niacin

% CALORIES FROM: protein 11%, fat 9%, carbohydrate 80%

Hot Cran-Apple Cider

 The inviting aromas of spices fill the air while this warming drink simmers on the stove. It will delight people of all ages after a skating party or autumn walk, or taken along in a thermos on a winter outing.

1/2 teaspoon cinnamon

Pinch each ground nutmeg, cloves, and allspice

2 cups cranberry juice

2 cups apple juice

In small jar with lid, combine cinnamon, nutmeg, cloves, and allspice with 1/4 cup of the cranberry juice. Close lid and shake vigorously until blended. Pour into pot and add remaining cranberry and apple juice. Heat just to boiling.

Makes 4 servings, each 1 cup

PER SERVING: calories: 132, protein: 0.1 g, carbohydrate: 33 g, fat: 0.3 g, dietary fiber: 0.4 g, sodium: 7 mg

EXCELLENT SOURCE OF: vitamin C

% CALORIES FROM: protein 1%, fat 2%, carbohydrate 97%

Soy Milk Cappuccino

This is a healthy, delicious alternative to the '90s café choice. Experiment with different coffee substitutes or cocoa, then cozy up with your partner or a good book on a cold night.

1 cup soy milk

2 teaspoons maple syrup, brown sugar, or honey

2 teaspoons grain beverage powder (such as Pero or Roma) or unsweetened cocoa powder

1/4 teaspoon vanilla extract

Pinch ground cinnamon

Chocolate shavings (optional)

Heat soy milk to just below boiling in saucepan over medium-high heat or in microwave on high for 2 minutes. Remove from heat. Stir in maple syrup, grain beverage powder, vanilla, and cinnamon and beat with egg beater until frothy. Pour into mug and garnish with chocolate shavings (if using).

Makes one 1-cup serving

PER CUP: calories 110, protein: 6 g, carbohydrate: 16 g, fat: 3 g, dietary fiber: 0, Sodium: 171 mg

EXCELLENT SOURCE OF: calcium, riboflavin, vitamin D*
GOOD SOURCE OF: zinc, vitamin B_{12}*

% CALORIES FROM: protein 20%, fat 24%, carbohydrate 56%

*Analyzed using fortified ProSoya So Nice original soy beverage. Nutrient data will vary with other brands.

Fresh Fruit Salad

Starting the day with the tang of grapefruit and the zing of orange can be uplifting and awakening. Packed with vitamin C, fresh fruit offers protection against environmental stresses. Vary this salad with fruits of the seasons or frozen blueberries. Treat yourself to organic fruits whenever possible.

1 banana, peeled and sliced	1 pear, chopped
1 grapefruit, peeled and sectioned	1/2 cup orange juice
1 apple, chopped	Sprig fresh mint, chopped (optional)

Combine chopped fruit in bowl. Pour orange juice over fruit. Garnish with mint (if using).

Makes 2 servings, each serving 1 1/4 cups

PER SERVING: calories 199, protein: 2 g, carbohydrate: 49 g, fat: 1 g, dietary fiber: 6 g, sodium: 3 mg

EXCELLENT SOURCE OF: vitamin C
GOOD SOURCE OF: folate, magnesium, potassium

% CALORIES FROM: protein 4%, fat 4%, carbohydrate 92%

Good Morning Granola

 This granola can be baked in the oven on baking trays, in a roasting pan, or in a large 15-inch-diameter metal bowl. The results will give you a healthy, delicious and easy start to your days for a week or two. If you like, you may replace the maple syrup with an additional 1/2 cup apple juice concentrate.

1/2 cup apple juice concentrate

1/2 cup almond butter or tahini

1/2 cup maple syrup

1 teaspoon ground cinnamon

1 teaspoon vanilla or almond
  extract

8 cups rolled oats

1 cup chopped almonds or
  sunflower seeds (optional)

1 cup currants, raisins, or
  chopped dates

Preheat oven to 350°. Combine apple juice concentrate, almond butter, maple syrup, cinnamon, and vanilla in a bowl or blender. Mix well. Combine oats and almonds (if using) in a large bowl or roasting pan. Pour liquid mixture over oats and stir to coat evenly. Spread out evenly in the roasting pan, on baking trays, or up along the sides of a metal bowl. Bake for 20 minutes or until golden brown, stirring after 10 minutes to prevent burning. Cool, stir in fruit, and store in jar with lid or plastic bags.

Makes 11 cups

PER CUP: calories 397, protein: 12 g, carbohydrate: 67 g, fat: 11 g, dietary fiber: 8 g, sodium: 9 mg

EXCELLENT SOURCE OF: iron, magnesium, thiamin
GOOD SOURCE OF: potassium, zinc, niacin, riboflavin

% CALORIES FROM: protein 11%, fat 23%, carbohydrate 65%

Oatmeal Porridge

 In this eat-and-run age, having a bowl of cooked oats can be comforting and very soothing to the stomach. Flaxseed oil may sound like an unusual item to put on your cereal, but it's an old European tradition from the era when small opaque bottles of fresh pressed flaxseed oil were delivered every week by horse and wagon. Try it, and see if you like this way of getting your omega-3s!

2 cups water

1 cup rolled oats

2 tablespoons raisins or chopped dates

1/8 teaspoon ground cinnamon

1/4 cup soy, rice, or dairy milk

2-3 teaspoons maple syrup

2 teaspoons flaxseed oil (optional)

Bring water to boil in covered saucepan over high heat. Stir or whisk in rolled oats, raisins, and cinnamon. Reduce heat. Cover and simmer for 15 minutes (2 to 4 minutes if using quick-cooking oats), stirring occasionally. Transfer to serving bowl and garnish with milk, maple syrup, and flaxseed oil (if using).

Makes 2 servings, each serving 1 cup

PER CUP: calories 214, protein: 8 g, carbohydrate: 41 g, fat: 3 g, dietary fiber: 5 g, sodium: 15 mg
WITH FLAXSEED OIL: calories 235, fat 7.5 g

EXCELLENT SOURCE OF: thiamin (and omega-3s, with flaxseed oil)
GOOD SOURCE OF: iron, magnesium

% CALORIES FROM: protein 14%, fat 12%, carbohydrate 74%

WITH FLAXSEED OIL: % CALORIES FROM: protein 12%, fat 26%, carbohydrate 62%

Scrambled Tofu

A replacement for scrambled eggs in the morning, this no-cholesterol dish goes well with toast and juice or a hot beverage. It also makes an easy-to-assemble source of protein, vitamins, and minerals at lunch or dinner time.

1 pound firm tofu

1/2 cup sliced mushrooms

2 tablespoons chopped green onions

1/2 small clove garlic, minced

2 tablespoons vegetable stock or 1 1/2 teaspoons canola oil

1 teaspoon chopped fresh cilantro

1/4 teaspoon ground cumin

1/4 teaspoon salt

Pinch turmeric powder

1 tablespoon nutritional yeast (page 218)

1 tablespoon salsa (optional)

Press tofu for 20 minutes as described on page 220. Place tofu in bowl and mash with fork. Sauté mushrooms, green onions, and garlic in vegetable stock or oil in skillet over medium heat for 3 to 5 minutes or until the water has evaporated. Stir in tofu, cilantro, cumin, salt, and turmeric; sauté for 4 to 5 minutes. Stir in yeast and salsa (if using).

Makes 2 servings

PER SERVING: calories 191, protein: 21 g, carbohydrate: 7 g, fat: 11 g, dietary fiber: 1 g, sodium: 310 mg
WITH OIL: calories 220, fat: 14 g

EXCELLENT SOURCE OF: calcium (using tofu made with calcium), iron, folate, niacin, riboflavin, thiamin, vitamin B_{12} (using Red Star Vegetarian Support Formula Nutritional Yeast), omega-3 fatty acids
GOOD SOURCE OF: magnesium, potassium, zinc

% CALORIES FROM: protein 39%, fat 47%, carbohydrate 14%
WITH OIL: % CALORIES FROM: protein 34%, fat 54%, carbohydrate 12%

Dips, Spreads, and Snacks

Avocado Dip

 Many Mexican foods can be low in fat: black beans, chili beans, corn, tomato products, and tortilla shells. Avocados are an exception, adding a creamy, soothing, and colorful touch to a meal or festive occasion. Nutritional yeast packs extra punch into this dip that can be served with crackers, rice cakes, or baked tortilla chips.

2 ripe avocados

2-3 teaspoons lime juice

1/2 teaspoon tamari or soy sauce

1 teaspoon nutritional yeast
   (page 218)

1/4 teaspoon chili powder

1/4 teaspoon garlic powder

Pinch pepper

2 teaspoons chopped
   green onions

2 teaspoons chopped
   fresh cilantro

Scoop avocado flesh into bowl and mash until smooth. Blend in lime juice, tamari, yeast, chili powder, garlic powder, and pepper. Stir in onions and cilantro. Adjust seasoning.

Makes 1 cup

PER 1/4 CUP: calories 166, protein: 2 g, carbohydrate: 8 g, fat: 15 g, dietary fiber: 5 g, sodium: 54 mg

EXCELLENT SOURCE OF: riboflavin, thiamin, vitamin B6
GOOD SOURCE OF: magnesium, potassium, folate, niacin, vitamin C

% CALORIES FROM: protein 5%, fat 77%, carbohydrate 18%

Analyzed using Red Star Vegetarian Support Formula Nutritional Yeast

Black Bean Hummus

 The balance of protein, fat, and carbohydrate in this recipe is light and lean. Keep this very low fat dip or spread in your refrigerator as a quick snack to serve with carrot sticks, crackers, or bread. It's a great source of protein, trace minerals, and folate.

2 cups cooked or canned black turtle beans or regular black beans

2 tablespoons liquid from cooking beans or from can

2 tablespoons lemon juice

1 tablespoon tamari or soy sauce

1 clove garlic, chopped

1/2 teaspoon ground cumin

Pinch cayenne pepper

2 tablespoons chopped fresh parsley

Combine beans, liquid, lemon juice, tamari, garlic, cumin, and cayenne in food processor and purée until smooth. Add parsley and blend for 5 seconds.

Makes 1 1/2 cups

PER 1/2 CUP: calories 168, protein: 11 g, carbohydrate: 32 g, fat: 0.5 g, dietary fiber: 7 g, sodium: 341 mg

EXCELLENT SOURCE OF: iron, folate
GOOD SOURCE OF: magnesium, potassium, thiamin, vitamin C

% CALORIES FROM: protein 25%, fat 3%, carbohydrate 72%

Curry Sandwich Spread

This mild curry sandwich filling has the look and texture of egg salad. The recipe makes enough for four sandwiches or it can be served as an appetizer with raw vegetables, crackers, or bread.

1 pound firm tofu

1/4 cup tofu mayonnaise (page 111) or commercial mayonnaise

1 tablespoon chopped green onion

1 tablespoon chopped fresh parsley

2 teaspoons tamari or soy sauce

1/2 teaspoon curry powder

1/2 teaspoon chili powder

1/2 teaspoon nutritional yeast (page 218)

1/4 teaspoon garlic powder

Salt and pepper to taste

Press tofu for 20 minutes as described on page 220. Discard liquid. Mash tofu in bowl with fork. Stir in all remaining ingredients.

Makes 2 cups

PER 1/2 CUP: calories 188, protein: 20 g, carbohydrate: 8 g, fat: 10 g, dietary fiber: 3 g, sodium: 246 mg

EXCELLENT SOURCE OF: calcium*, iron, thiamin, omega-3 fatty acids
GOOD SOURCE OF: magnesium, zinc, folate, riboflavin, vitamin B6

% CALORIES FROM: protein 39%, fat 47%, carbohydrate 14%

*Analyzed using tofu set with calcium.

Gee Whiz Spread

Here's a tasty, nutrition packed, easy-to-make spread, without the saturated fat and cholesterol of cheese, from The Uncheese Cookbook, *by Joanne Stepaniak (published by the Book Publishing Company). It's great with veggie burgers to make "cheezeburgers," on crackers, and in sandwiches.*

1 1/2 cups great northern beans (cooked or 15-ounce can)

1/2 cup chopped pimiento or roasted bell pepper (page 83)

6 tablespoons nutritional yeast (page 218)

3 tablespoons fresh lemon juice

2-3 tablespoons tahini

1/2 teaspoon onion powder

1/2 teaspoon prepared yellow mustard

1/2 teaspoon salt

In food processor, blend beans, pimiento, yeast, lemon juice, tahini, onion, mustard, and salt until smooth. Chill thoroughly before serving.

Makes 2 cups

PER 1/2 CUP: calories 40, protein: 3 g, carbohydrate: 8 g, fat: 1 g, dietary fiber: 1 g, sodium: 77 mg

EXCELLENT SOURCE OF: zinc, folate, niacin, riboflavin, thiamin and vitamins B_6, B_{12}* and C

GOOD SOURCE OF: iron, magnesium, potassium

% CALORIES FROM: protein 27%, fat 26%, carbohydrate 47%

---

*Analyzed using Red Star Vegetarian Support Formula Nutritional Yeast

Gomasio

Sprinkled over vegetables, soups, or cooked grains and beans, Gomasio deepens the overall flavor of a dish. It is a perfect alternative to using salt at the table. Look for dulse or kelp powders at your local health food store.

1/2 cup hulled sesame seeds

1/2 teaspoon salt

1/4 teaspoon dulse or kelp powder, optional

NOTE: To grind this amount of seeds all at once, you need a mortar that has a 2-inch deep bowl and a 3 1/2-inch-wide mouth. If your mortar is smaller, crush seeds in batches. Alternatively, use a small electric grinder.

Dry-roast sesame seeds in a skillet over medium heat for 5 to 7 minutes, stirring frequently until seeds can be crushed between your thumb and finger. Transfer to mortar or food grinder. Add salt and dulse. Using pestle and grinding in a circular motion or using pulse action of the grinder, grind seeds until most of them are crushed (approximately 75 percent) and coated with their own oil. Store in a sealed jar in refrigerator for several weeks.

Makes 1/2 cup

PER 1/2 TEASPOON SERVING: calories 9, protein: 0.3 g, carbohydrate: 0.4 g, fat: 0.8 g dietary fiber: 0.2 g, sodium: 24 mg

% CALORIES FROM: protein 12%, fat 73%, carbohydrate 15%

Gooda Cheeze

 Gooda Cheeze is the clever creation of Joanne Stepaniak, author of the Uncheese Cookbook *and* Table for Two. *The agar dissolves after simmering for a few minutes, then cools, forming a firm mold, so that Gooda Cheeze can be sliced into wedges or slices. To learn more about the characteristics of agar, refer to page 217.*

1 3/4 cups water	3 tablespoons fresh lemon juice
1/2 cup chopped carrot	1 tablespoon Dijon mustard
1/3 cup agar flakes or 2 teaspoons agar powder (page 217)	2 teaspoons onion powder
1/2 cup unsalted raw cashew pieces	1 teaspoon salt
1/4 cup nutritional yeast (page 218)	1/2 teaspoon garlic powder
3 tablespoons tahini	1/2 teaspoon dry mustard
	1/4 teaspoon turmeric
	1/4 teaspoon paprika
	1/4 teaspoon ground cumin

In covered saucepan, bring water, carrots, and agar to boil. Lower heat and simmer 10 minutes or until the agar is dissolved. Pour carrot mixture into blender and add cashews, yeast, tahini, lemon juice, mustard, onion powder, salt, garlic powder, mustard, turmeric, paprika, and cumin, processing until very smooth. Pour immediately into lightly oiled 3-cup bowl or mold with rounded bottom. Cover and chill several hours or overnight. To serve, turn out of mold and slice into wedges.

Makes 3 cups

PER 1/4 CUP SERVING: calories 70, protein: 3 g, carbohydrate: 5 g, fat: 5 g, dietary fiber: 0.9 g, sodium: 296 mg

EXCELLENT SOURCE OF: niacin, riboflavin, thiamin, vitamin B_6
GOOD SOURCE OF: folate, vitamin A and B_{12}*

% CALORIES FROM: protein 15%, fat 59%, carbohydrate 26%

---

*Analyzed using Red Star Vegetarian Support Formula Nutritional Yeast

Note that although the percentage of calories from fat appears high, the total calories and grams of fat per serving are fairly low, about half those of dairy-based Gouda cheese.

Hummus

Hummus, or the lower-fat Black Bean Hummus (page 73) , can be a staple and perhaps even rival your jar of peanut butter. It is a thoroughly nourishing spread to keep near the front of the refrigerator for hungry children and teens.

2 cups cooked chick-peas
 (reserve liquid)

1/3 cup tahini

1/3 cup lemon juice

1/3 cup cooking water from
 the chick-peas

1-2 cloves garlic, chopped

1 1/2 teaspoons ground cumin

1/2 teaspoon salt (less if using
 canned beans)

Pinch cayenne pepper

3 tablespoons chopped fresh
 parsley

1-2 tablespoons extra-virgin
 olive oil (optional)

In food processor, combine chick-peas, tahini, lemon juice, cooking water, garlic, cumin, salt, and cayenne. Purée until smooth, occasionally scraping down sides of bowl. Add parsley and olive oil (if using), and blend for 30 seconds. Adjust seasoning.

VERY LOW FAT VARIATION: Omit tahini and oil; reduce lemon juice and cooking liquid to 3 tablespoons each.

Makes 2 1/2 cups

PER 1/2 CUP SERVING: calories 213, protein: 10 g, carbohydrate: 23 g, fat: 11 g, dietary fiber: 7 g, sodium: 240 mg VERY LOW FAT VARIATION: calories 114, fat 2 g

EXCELLENT SOURCE OF: magnesium, folate, thiamin
GOOD SOURCE OF: iron, zinc, vitamin C

% CALORIES FROM: protein 16%, fat 43%, carbohydrate 41%

VERY LOW FAT VARIATION: % CALORIES FROM: protein 20%, fat 14%, carbohydrate 65%

Morocc-Un-Butter

Here's a spicy North African spread without the cholesterol or trans fatty acids of butter or margarine. It is delicious on crusty bread as an accompaniment to the Spicy Eggplant Soup on page 122. The base is tahini, a sesame seed butter. Some brands of tahini are drier than others: if you find that your butter is too stiff, add a tablespoon or more of hot water to thin.

1/2 cup tahini

3–4 tablespoons lemon juice

3 tablespoons chopped green onions

2 tablespoons chopped fresh parsley

2 tablespoons chopped fresh cilantro

1–2 cloves garlic

1 1/2 teaspoons ground cumin

1 teaspoon paprika

1 teaspoon tamari or soy sauce

1/4 teaspoon chili powder or fresh chili paste (optional)

In food processor, combine tahini, lemon juice, onions, parsley, cilantro, garlic, cumin, paprika, tamari, and chili (if using). Blend until smooth.

Makes 1 cup

PER TABLESPOON: calories 48, protein: 2 g, carbohydrate: 2 g, fat: 4 g, dietary fiber: 1 g, sodium: 22 mg

% CALORIES FROM: protein 11%, fat 74%, carbohydrate 15%

Note that in butter and margarine, all of the calories are from fat.

Pesto-the-Best-Oh!

This pesto is absolutely delicious. It was developed by Valerie McIntyre, a significant contributor to the co-housing community in which Vesanto lives. The spread delivers the rich flavors of basil and garlic for a gourmet appetizer on a crisp bread or for a family treat on pasta. You must use fresh-tasting walnuts; rancid nuts will overpower the other ingredients. This recipe can be mild or eye-watering, depending on the amount of garlic used. When basil and garlic are in season, make lots of pesto and freeze in cup-size mounds on a baking tray, then wrap in wax paper and store in plastic bags in your freezer for year-round pleasure.

1 cup walnuts	2 tablespoons Bragg's liquid
4 cups basil, lightly packed leaves	amino acids or tamari or
and tender stems	soy sauce
1/4 cup olive oil	3-6 cloves garlic
2 tablespoons (or less) lemon	1/8 teaspoon black pepper
juice	

In food processor, blend walnuts until fine; remove from food processor. Combine basil, oil, lemon juice, Bragg's liquid, garlic, and pepper in food processor; blend until smooth. Add the ground walnuts and blend until smooth.

FOR USE WITH PASTA: Combine 1/2 cup pesto with 1/3 cup stock or water. Blend to make a sauce. Stir into 4 cups cooked pasta. Add Bragg's seasoning or tamari to taste.

Makes 1 1/3 cups

PER TABLESPOON: calories 63, protein: 1 g, carbohydrate: 2 g, fat: 6 g, dietary fiber: 0.6 g, sodium: 87 mg*

EXCELLENT SOURCE OF: omega-3 fatty acids

% CALORIES FROM: protein 6%, fat 84%, carbohydrate 10%

*Analyzed using tamari.

Raw Vegetable Platter

Serve a platter filled with colorful, cut up vegetables:

- to encourage your family to eat their veggies when they come in from school or work
- as an attractive way of serving any of these foods at mealtimes
- as a low-cal, healthy snack while watching TV
- as an artistic accompaniment to festive meals
- as a great way to get vitamins, antioxidants, phytochemicals, and fiber

Here's a list of raw veggies you can serve on their own or with one of the dips or spreads in this chapter:

- asparagus tips
- broccoli florets
- carrot sticks
- cauliflower florets
- celery sticks
- cherry tomatoes
- cucumber disks
- green beans
- green onions
- jicama sticks
- kohlrabi sticks
- mushrooms
- parsnip sticks
- red, yellow, and green pepper strips
- snow peas
- sweet potato strips (dipped in water with a little lemon juice to prevent browning)
- turnip strips
- zucchini strips

Roasted Garlic and Yam Spread

 This fat-free spread is packed with the protective antioxidant beta-carotene, also known as vitamin A. Its deep orange color makes it very attractive served with crackers, vegetable sticks, or assorted breads such as pumpernickel, rye, wheat, or sourdough.

2–3 cloves garlic, peeled

3 small yams, peeled and sliced, about 4 cups

1 1/2 teaspoons lemon juice

1 teaspoon nutritional yeast (page 218)

1/2 teaspoon oregano

1/4 teaspoon salt

Pinch black pepper

1 tablespoon chopped fresh parsley

Preheat oven to 300°. Roast garlic for 25 to 30 minutes until soft and golden. Steam yam slices until soft. Transfer garlic and yams to food processor. Add lemon juice, yeast, oregano, salt and pepper; purée until smooth. Add parsley and purée for 5 seconds.

Makes 1 1/2 cups

PER 1/3 RECIPE: calories 97, protein: 2 g, carbohydrate: 23 g, fat: 0.2 g, dietary fiber: 3 g, sodium: 204 mg

EXCELLENT SOURCE OF: niacin, riboflavin, thiamin, vitamins A, B6, C

% CALORIES FROM: protein 8%, fat 1%, carbohydrate 91%

Roasted Red Bell Peppers

 Roasting bell peppers accentuates the sweetness of the naturally oc-curring sugars of the vegetable. The charring that occurs when they are roasted adds a slight smoky flavor. Roasted peppers can replace pimientos in the recipe for Gee Whiz, page 75. Roasted peppers can also be cut into strips and served on a platter with a drizzle of extra-virgin olive or flaxseed oil, fresh herbs, and a splash of lemon juice or balsamic vinegar. Cut them into julienne strips and use as a topping for the Veggie Pepperoni Pizza, page 158. They could be diced and introduced to the Cumin and Currant Pilaf, page 169, or sliced and added to the Sushi, page 150.

Choose peppers that have even surfaces rather than those that are curved and gnarly. Wash and set the peppers on the top rack directly under broiler heat. Turn them occasionally with a pair of tongs until they begin to char, about 5 to 8 minutes. Remove from oven, transfer the peppers to a bowl, and cover with a plastic bag so the peppers steam. This will make peeling the peppers easier once they are cool enough to handle. With a paring knife, remove the skin from the peppers, cut off the top, slice the pepper in half, and remove the seeds. Cut peppers into strips and use according to the chosen recipe. Peppers will keep for 2 to 3 days in the refrigerator.

VARIATION: Try yellow or orange bell peppers in place of red peppers.

Toasted Sunflower Seeds

 These seeds make a savory alternative to potato or corn chips. Easy to make, they are a good snack for hungry children at home, on the trail, or at the lake. They can also be used as a garnish for salads, baked potatoes, and cooked grains.

2 cups sunflower seeds

2 tablespoons nutritional yeast
   (page 218)

2 teaspoons tamari or
   soy sauce

Preheat oven to 350°. Spread seeds evenly on baking sheet and bake for 10 to 12 minutes. Transfer seeds to a large bowl, stir in yeast and tamari, and toss to coat evenly. Let cool before transferring to jar with lid. Seeds keep for 1 week on the shelf or 2 to 3 weeks refrigerated (if they are around that long!).

Makes 2 cups

PER TABLESPOON: calories 48, protein: 2 g, carbohydrate: 2 g, fat: 4 g, dietary fiber: 0.9 g, sodium: 21 mg
GOOD SOURCE OF: riboflavin, thiamin, vitamin B_6

% CALORIES FROM: protein 14%, fat 70%, carbohydrate 16%

What Will I Spread on My Bread or Toast?

Which is the lesser of two evils, butter or margarine? If you've become tired of this debate, opt for a spread that can offer some nutritional pluses found in neither. For example, almond butter and Curry Sandwich Spread are tasty sources of calcium. Cashew butter provides you with zinc. Gee Whiz Spread, Black Bean Hummus, the very low fat variation on Hummus, and Roasted Garlic and Yam Spread are high in nutritional value, yet low in calories. And all of the recipes listed below offer wonderfully satisfying flavor.

- Almond butter, cashew butter, and other nut and seed butters
- Avocado Dip (page 72)
- Curry Sandwich Spread (page 74)
- Fruit Jam
- Gee Whiz Spread (page 75)
- Gooda Cheeze (page 77)
- Hummus (page 78)
- Hummus: very low fat variation (page 79)
- Miso, thinly spread
- Morocc-Un-Butter (page 79)
- Pesto-the Best-Oh! (page 80)
- Roasted Garlic and Yam Spread (page 82)
- Sesame Tahini with blackstrap molasses or honey (a thin layer of each)

Salads

Apple Walnut Salad

 This is a pretty salad for festive occasions, or even to cheer you up on a rainy day! The salad is a mound of lettuce, sprouts, peppers, and apple slices surrounded by a circle of orange slices and walnuts.
Serve it with Orange Mint Dressing (page 107) or with Raspberry Vinaigrette (page 109). The salad provides half your day's supply of omega-3 fatty acids.

1/3 red bell pepper

1/3 green bell pepper

1/2 small red apple

1 tablespoon lemon juice

5 cups leafy green lettuce, torn
   into bite-sized pieces

1 cup alfalfa sprouts

1 orange, peeled and thinly
   sliced crosswise

1/2 cup walnut halves

Cut top and bottom from peppers, remove seeds, and cut peppers lengthwise into 1/4-inch strips. Slice apple into quarters, then core and cut lengthwise into 1/4-inch slices. Toss in lemon juice to keep from turning brown. Toss lettuce, peppers, and sprouts together in large bowl. Form a mound of tossed salad on large platter. Arrange orange slices and walnuts around base of salad. Garnish salad with apple slices.

Makes 4 servings

PER 2-CUP SERVING: calories 125, protein: 4 g, carbohydrate: 13 g, fat: 8 g, dietary fiber: 4 g, sodium: 8 mg

EXCELLENT SOURCE OF: vitamin C, omega-3 fatty acids
GOOD SOURCE OF: folate, vitamin A

% Calories from: protein 10%, fat 53%, carbohydrate 37%

For maximum freshness...

For maximum freshness of walnuts and the valuable omega-3 fatty acids they contain, purchase these nuts in the shell or from stores that refrigerate the walnut pieces. Store cracked nuts in your freezer.

Basmati Rice Salad

Basmati is an aromatic rice grown in the foothills of the Himalayas. Sweet raisins, mild curry, and the nutty taste of basmati rice colorfully combine to make a truly delicious salad. For the quick-cooking version described here, you may use white basmati rice, or use the longer-cooking brown basmati as described in the variation.

3 tablespoons raisins

1/3 cup hot water

1 3/4 cups water

1 cup white basmati rice

1/2 teaspoon salt

1/8 teaspoon turmeric powder

3 tablespoons soaking water
  from raisins

2 tablespoons mild curry paste

2 tablespoons lemon juice

1/4 cup finely diced sweet red
  pepper

2 tablespoons chopped parsley

1 teaspoon coriander seed,
  crushed

Soak raisins in 1/3 cup hot water for 30 minutes. Bring 1 3/4 cups water to boil. Pour in rice, salt, and turmeric. Cover, reduce heat to simmer, and cook for 20 minutes. Transfer rice to medium bowl and allow to cool. Combine raisin water, curry paste, and lemon juice and mix well. Stir curry mixture into rice, along with red pepper, parsley, and coriander seed, until curry color is evenly distributed. Drain liquid from raisins and add raisins to rice. Gently mix with fork.

VARIATION: Use brown basmati rice in place of white and cook for 45 minutes in 2 cups water.

Makes 4 servings

PER SERVING: calories 245, protein: 3 g, carbohydrate: 54 g, fat: 4 g, dietary fiber: 3 g, sodium: 297 mg

EXCELLENT SOURCE OF: vitamin C
GOOD SOURCE OF: iron, thiamin

% CALORIES FROM: protein 5%, fat 13%, carbohydrate 82%

Caesar Salad

 Here's a healthier version of a perennial favorite. Drying the lettuce leaves as much as possible after washing serves two functions. It lets the dressing cling to the leaves, and it removes water that would otherwise dilute a very flavorful dressing. You may purchase croutons made with or without oil for use in the salad (check labels).

Dressing

12-ounce package soft silken tofu

3 cloves garlic

5 tablespoons lemon juice

2 tablespoons capers

4 teaspoons Dijon mustard

1/2 teaspoon salt

1/8 teaspoon freshly cracked black pepper

2 tablespoons extra-virgin olive oil (optional)

Drain water from tofu package and place tofu in a food processor or blender. Add garlic, lemon juice, capers, mustard, salt, and pepper, and purée until smooth. If using oil, pour in very slowly. Adjust seasoning.

Makes 2 cups dressing

Salad

1 head romaine lettuce (8 cups)

1 1/2 cups croutons

1/2 cup Caesar dressing

2–4 tablespoons grated soy or dairy Parmesan cheese

Cut romaine into bite-size pieces (1-inch square). Rinse lettuce in cold water and spin or pat dry with a clean tea towel. Place lettuce in large bowl and toss with croutons and dressing until lettuce is coated. Sprinkle with cheese.

PER SERVING: calories 82, protein: 6 g, carbohydrate: 12 g, fat: 1 g, dietary fiber: 2 g, sodium: 356 mg
WITH OIL IN CROUTONS & DRESSING: calories 129, fat 6 g

% CALORIES FROM: protein 28%, fat 15%, carbohydrate 56%
WITH OIL IN CROUTONS & DRESSING: % CALORIES FROM: protein 18%, fat 39%, carbohydrate 43%

Basic analysis using Kellogg's Croutettes Croutons (nonfat) and Soymage Parmesan Cheese Alternative.

Calcium-Rich Greens

 Kale can be eaten both raw, as in this recipe, and steamed. When eaten raw, it is best sliced very thin, due to its fibrous nature. In this salad, which provides 135 milligrams calcium per 50-calorie portion, kale is combined with napa cabbage (also known as Chinese cabbage or sui choy) and broccoli, two other greens chosen for their high calcium availability. The nutritional analysis shows that a substantial proportion of the calories in greens are from protein; the fat present is beneficial plant oils. Folate, a vitamin needed for cell division and especially valuable during pregnancy, is related to the word foliage, and is present in substantial amounts in greens. Oriental Dressing (page 108) or Lemon Tahini Dressing (page 106) complements this salad.

2 cups kale

2 cups Chinese cabbage

2 1/2 cups broccoli florets and peeled, sliced stems

1 cup diced sweet red pepper

Remove kale from stem and slice leaves matchstick thin. Cut cabbage leaves in half lengthwise and slice into 1/2-inch strips. Combine kale, Chinese cabbage, broccoli, and red pepper.

Makes 4 servings

PER 2-CUP SERVING: calories 50, protein: 4 g, carbohydrate: 10 g, fat: 0.6 g, dietary fiber: 3 g, sodium: 59 mg

EXCELLENT SOURCE OF: vitamins A and C
GOOD SOURCE OF: calcium, potassium, folate, vitamin B6

% CALORIES FROM: protein 24%, fat 9%, carbohydrate 67%

Couscous Salad

 Couscous, sometimes known as "Moroccan pasta," is made from durum wheat that has had the bran and germ removed, been coarsely ground, and precooked. Dishes using this refined wheat product are very quick to prepare. Here it is colorfully combined with currants, sweet red pepper, and parsley.

1/4 cup currants

1/4 cup hot water

I cup couscous

I cup water

1/2 teaspoon salt

I tablespoon tahini

I tablespoon lemon juice

1/4 cup finely diced red bell pepper

2 tablespoons chopped fresh parsley

1/2 teaspoon coriander seeds, crushed

1/2 teaspoon ground cumin

Pinch pepper

Soak currants in 1/4 cup hot water for 10 to 15 minutes. Meanwhile, measure couscous into bowl. Bring water and salt to boil, then pour over couscous. Cover bowl with plate to keep in steam and set aside to cool completely. Mix tahini and lemon juice together in small bowl; stir into couscous. Drain currants and add to couscous along with diced red pepper, parsley, coriander, cumin, and pepper. Gently toss with fork.

Makes 4 servings

PER 3/4-CUP SERVING: calories 200, protein: 6 g, carbohydrate: 39 g, fat: 2 g, dietary fiber: 3 g, sodium: 300 mg

EXCELLENT SOURCE OF: vitamin C
GOOD SOURCE OF: thiamin

% CALORIES FROM: protein 12%, fat 11%, carbohydrate 77%

David's Garden of Plenty Salad

 Vesanto's husband, David, spends half an hour several times a week assembling this salad. Stored in a couple of large, well-sealed containers (such as Tupperware), it will last for 3 or 4 days. In this case, the romaine is best added fresh every 2 days. Alternately, this recipe will also feed a big hungry family gathering. It is excellent with Oriental Dressing (page 108), Lemon Tahini Dressing (page 106), or Raspberry Vinaigrette (page 109).

5 large leaves kale	I stalk broccoli
5 large leaves romaine	1/2 small head cauliflower
5 leaves napa (Chinese) cabbage	3–4 carrots
1/4 head red cabbage	I sweet red pepper

Remove stem from kale and cut kale into matchsticks. Tear lettuce into bite-size pieces. Cut napa cabbage leaves in half lengthwise, and slice into 1/4-inch strips. Slice red cabbage into thin slices. Cut broccoli and cauliflower into bite-size florets. Broccoli stem can be peeled and diced. Slice carrots and cut red pepper into 1/4-inch strips. Toss all in bowl.

Makes 10 servings

PER 2-CUP SERVING: calories 47, protein: 3 g, carbohydrate: 10 g, fat: 0.4 g, dietary fiber: 3 g, sodium: 33 mg

EXCELLENT SOURCE OF: folate, vitamins A and C
GOOD SOURCE OF: potassium, vitamin B6

% CALORIES FROM: protein 21%, fat 7%, carbohydrate, 72%

Deep Green Leafy Salad

 The contrasting colors in this salad—light green lettuce, dark green kale, and bright red pepper strips—make a lovely presentation tossed in a bowl or served on a platter, accompanied by any of the dressings in this book. You'll see in the analysis that salad vegetables provide about 10 percent calories from fat. However, these calories include the beneficial plant oils, high in healthful omega-3 fatty acids.

4 cups torn leafy lettuce

3–4 cups thinly sliced kale

1 cup grated carrot

1/2 each sweet red and yellow
  peppers

1/2 cup grated red radish
  (optional)

2 cups alfalfa sprouts

Wash lettuce, spin-dry, and tear into bite-size pieces. Place in large bowl. Remove kale leaves from stem, and slice leaves matchstick thin. Discard stems and add leaves to bowl. Seed red and yellow peppers. Cut into 1/4-inch strips. Set aside for garnish one-third of the pepper strips, grated carrots, and radishes (if using); add remainder to bowl and toss. Garnish top of salad with reserved peppers, carrots, and radishes. Arrange alfalfa sprouts around edge.

Makes 4 to 6 servings

PER 1/4 RECIPE: calories 60, protein: 4 g, carbohydrate: 12 g, fat: 0.8 g, dietary fiber: 4 g, sodium: 38 mg

EXCELLENT SOURCE OF: vitamins A and C
GOOD SOURCE OF: iron, calcium, potassium, folate, vitamin B6, omega-3 fatty acids

% CALORIES FROM: protein 20%, fat 10%, carbohydrate 70%

Fresh Vegetable Salad Roll

 After the ingredients for this salad roll are laid out before you, the rolls can be assembled with ease. Different sauces, such as Spicy Peanut (page 190), Lemon Tahini (page 106), Teriyaki (page 192), barbecue, or plum, inside the roll as well as for dipping, create a deliciously wide range of flavor possibilities. Annie's Barbecue Sauce (from a Vermont-based company) is an outstanding low-fat product. Try experimenting with different ingredients for the filling such as replacing avocado with Crispy Tofu Fingers (page 132).

1 sheet rice paper (8 1/2 inches)

8 cups warm water in large bowl

1/3 cup cooked brown rice

1 teaspoon sauce (peanut, barbecue, etc.)

2 tablespoons grated carrot

3 slices avocado

6-inch strip green onion, sliced lengthwise

1/2 teaspoon chopped fresh cilantro

1/2 teaspoon julienned pickled gingerroot (optional)

Dip one sheet of rice paper into water for 5 seconds, then place on cutting board. Pat with dry cloth to absorb any excess water. Spread rice on paper in a square, leaving 1-inch border on all sides. Layer sauce, carrot, avocado, green onion, cilantro, and ginger along bottom portion of rice. Fold right and left margins toward the center followed by the bottom margin. Moisten top margin of paper. Using both hands, tightly roll the paper toward the top. Apply a bit of pressure with hands to seal roll.

Makes one roll

PER ROLL, WITHOUT DIPPING SAUCE: calories 146, protein: 3 g, carbohydrate: 23 g, fat: 5 g, dietary fiber: 3 g, sodium: 34 mg

EXCELLENT SOURCE OF: vitamin A
GOOD SOURCE OF: magnesium, niacin, thiamin, vitamin B6

% CALORIES FROM: protein 8%, fat 35%, carbohydrate 57%

Pickled Beet and Kale Salad

 The beets are brightened by the presence of vinegar, resulting in a pleasing contrast of red and green in this salad. Balsamic vinegar is an excellent choice; however, raspberry, red wine, or apple cider vinegar is delightful as well. The pickled beets are also good served without the kale, and will keep in the refrigerator for up to 4 days.

4 fresh beets

1/4 cup balsamic vinegar

1/4 teaspoon caraway seeds

1/4 teaspoon salt

Pinch clove powder

4 cups chopped kale

1 tablespoon chopped fresh
  parsley (optional)

Pinch freshly ground pepper

Cover beets with cold water in a pot. Bring to boil. Reduce heat to simmer and cook 20 to 40 minutes (depending on size) or until a thin skewer easily slips out of beet when pierced. Allow beets to cool in cooking liquid. Peel beets under cold running water by squeezing skins so they slip off. Slice beets; place in bowl and add vinegar, caraway seeds, salt, and cloves. Set aside for at least one hour in refrigerator, tossing to mix occasionally. Remove stems from kale. Discard stems and slice leaves very thin. Steam over medium-high heat for 3 minutes. Spread warm greens on serving platter and arrange beets over top. Garnish with parsley (if using) and pepper.

Makes 4 servings

PER SERVING: calories 77, protein: 3 g, carbohydrate: 16 g, fat: 0.6 g, dietary fiber: 3 g, sodium: 218 mg

EXCELLENT SOURCE OF: vitamins A, C
GOOD SOURCE OF: calcium, iron, potassium folate, vitamin B6

% CALORIES FROM: protein 17%, fat 7%, carbohydrate 76%

Potato Dill Salad

 Compare the nutritional analysis when this potato salad is made with the Tofu Mayonnaise on page 111 and with regular commercial mayonnaise.

4 unpeeled potatoes

1/3 cup mayonnaise (tofu or commercial)

2 tablespoons diced celery

2 tablespoons chopped green onions

2 tablespoons chopped fresh parsley

1 teaspoon Dijon mustard

1/2 teaspoon dillweed

1/4 teaspoon paprika

1/4 teaspoon salt

Pinch pepper

In a pot of boiling water, cook potatoes over medium heat for 20 minutes or until tender. Drain and cool under cold running water. Stir together mayonnaise, celery, onions, parsley, mustard, dill, paprika, salt, and pepper in bowl. Cube potatoes; stir into mayonnaise mixture and gently toss with fork.

VARIATION: Add one or two diced garlic dill pickles.

Make 4 servings

PER SERVING USING TOFU MAYO: calories: 118, protein: 4 g, carbohydrate: 25 g, fat: 0.8 g, dietary fiber: 2 g, sodium: 233 mg,
USING REGULAR COMMERCIAL MAYO: Calories 256, Fat 15 g

EXCELLENT SOURCE OF: potassium, vitamin C (even after the potatoes are cooked!)
GOOD SOURCE OF: niacin, thiamin, vitamin B_6

USING TOFU MAYO: % CALORIES FROM: protein 13%, fat 6%, carbohydrate 80%
USING REGULAR COMMERCIAL MAYO: % CALORIES FROM: protein 4%, fat 52%, carbohydrate 44%

Quinoa Salad with Lime Dressing

 Quinoa (pronounced keen-wa*) is an ancient grain, native to the high Andes regions of South America, and recently introduced to North America. It is often called a supergrain because of its excellent protein content and nutritional profile. In nature, quinoa is coated with a slightly bitter resin, which can be removed by rinsing. Most commercial quinoa has been prerinsed, however for certainty, wash the grain using a fine sieve until the rinse water is no longer foamy.*

1 1/2 cups water

1 cup quinoa

1/2 cup peeled, seeded, and
   diced cucumber

1/2 cup corn kernels (fresh,
   canned, or frozen)

1/4 cup diced sweet red pepper

2 tablespoons finely chopped
   green onion

4 teaspoons finely chopped
   cilantro

Bring water to a boil. Add quinoa, cover, lower heat, and simmer for 15 to 20 minutes or until water is absorbed. Let cool. In bowl, combine quinoa, cucumber, corn, red pepper, green onion, and cilantro.

Lime Dressing

3 tablespoons lime juice

3 tablespoons canola oil

1/2 teaspoon toasted sesame oil

1/2 teaspoon salt

Pinch pepper

In small bowl combine lime juice, canola oil, sesame oil, salt, and pepper. Pour over quinoa mixture and toss gently with fork. Adjust seasoning. Refrigerate for 1 to 3 hours before serving to let flavors blend.

Makes 4 servings

PER SERVING: calories: 276, protein: 6 g, carbohydrate: 35 g, fat 13 g, dietary fiber: 2 g, sodium: 139 mg

EXCELLENT SOURCE OF: iron, magnesium, and omega-3 fatty acids
GOOD SOURCE OF: potassium, zinc, riboflavin, vitamins C and E

% CALORIES FROM: protein 9%, fat 42%, carbohydrate 49%

Sun-Dried Tomato and Rice Salad

 When tomatoes are dried, they develop a wonderful sweetness and tang. Keep a little bag of them in your kitchen cupboard and they will often come in handy to add flavor and color to grains, salads, dressings, pastas, and many other dishes.

1/4 cup dry sun-dried tomatoes

4 cups cooked brown rice, cooled

1/4 cup tomato sauce

2 tablespoons sunflower seeds

2 tablespoons chopped parsley

2 tablespoons extra-virgin olive oil

2 tablespoons lemon juice

2 teaspoons chopped fresh basil

1/4 teaspoon garlic powder

1/4 teaspoon salt

Pinch black pepper

Soak tomatoes in 1/2 cup boiling water for 30 minutes or until soft; drain well and chop. In medium bowl combine rice, sun-dried tomatoes, tomato sauce, sunflower seeds, and parsley. In small bowl mix olive oil, lemon juice, basil, garlic powder, salt, and pepper. Pour over rice and gently toss with fork. Adjust seasoning to taste.

Makes 4 servings

PER SERVING: calories: 318, carbohydrate: 51g, protein: 6g, fat: 11g, sodium: 312 mg

EXCELLENT SOURCE OF: magnesium
GOOD SOURCE OF: iron, potassium, zinc, niacin, thiamin, Vitamins B6, C, and E

% CALORIES FROM: protein 8%, fat 29%, carbohydrate 63%

Thai Pasta Salad

 When vegetables are blanched in simmering water, their colors become brighter and deeper, and their texture becomes softer to the bite resulting in a texture referred to as "al dente." To blanch several different vegetables in the same pot, start with the vegetables that take the longest to cook (carrots and cauliflower), progressively adding the other vegetables in order of their densities, finishing with the snow peas, and heat until they are firm to the bite but not entirely cooked. Drain the water and immediately place under cold running water or in ice water to arrest the cooking and to preserve the color.

4 cups cooked pasta spirals
  (2 cups raw)
1 cup sliced carrots
1 cup cauliflower florets
1 cup diced sweet red pepper
1 cup snow peas, trimmed and
  sliced

1/2 cup sliced water chestnuts
  (optional)
2 tablespoons chopped green
  onions
1/2 cup Spicy Peanut Sauce
  (page 190)

Cook pasta according to the directions on the package. Drain under cold water; set aside. Blanch carrots, cauliflower, peppers, and snow peas until tender-crisp. (Blanching is not necessary if you prefer raw vegetables.) Plunge under cold water, drain, and add to thoroughly drained noodles. Add water chestnuts, green onions, and Peanut Sauce; toss until noodles are well coated.

Makes 4 servings

PER SERVING: calories 304, protein: 12 g, carbohydrate: 51 g, fat: 6 g, dietary fiber: 6 g, sodium: 614 mg

EXCELLENT SOURCE OF: niacin, thiamin, vitamins A and C
GOOD SOURCE OF: iron, magnesium, potassium, folate, riboflavin, and vitamin B_6 (and zinc using whole wheat pasta)

% CALORIES FROM: protein 15%, fat 19%, carbohydrate 66%

Watercress, Avocado, and Grapefruit Salad

The dressing for this elegant salad uses mirin—a Japanese rice wine that is subtle, delicious, and clean on the palate. The grapefruit juice can be squeezed from the remaining pulp after the segments are removed from the fruit.

1/3 bunch watercress

2 ripe avocados

1 grapefruit

Wash and dry watercress; arrange 3 to 4 stems on top third of 4 plates. Set aside. Cut avocados in half lengthwise and remove pits. Carefully remove pulp from each half in one piece using a soup spoon.

To fan avocado, make thin strips lengthwise starting 1/2-inch down from narrow end through to the bottom. With pressure from hand and at a 45 degree angle, push avocado so that it fans out. Arrange avocado fan on bed of greens so that the fanned area is near the bottom of the plate.

Slice top and bottom from grapefruit. Using sharp knife, slice skin and pith away to expose fruit. Cut along both sides of segments towards center to loosen them and remove. Garnish each plate with 2 segments to form an x on either side of the avocado.

Dressing

2 tablespoons grapefruit juice

2 tablespoons mirin

2 teaspoons rice vinegar

1/2 teaspoon tamari or soy sauce

1/2 teaspoon Gomasio (page 76), optional

Squeeze juice from pulp into small bowl. Combine juice, mirin, vinegar, and tamari. Spoon 1 tablespoon of dressing on each salad. Sprinkle each salad with pinch of Gomasio (if using).

Makes 4 servings

PER SERVING: calories 182, protein: 3 g, carbohydrate: 12 g, fat: 15 g, dietary fiber: 5 g, sodium: 15 mg

EXCELLENT SOURCE OF: vitamin C
GOOD SOURCE OF: magnesium, folate, niacin, thiamin, vitamins A and B_6

% CALORIES FROM: protein 5%, fat 64%, carbohydrate 28%

Dressings

Cucumber Dill Dressing

 In the heat of summer, cucumbers are so blessedly cooling. Serve this dressing with tender leafy greens and vine-ripened tomatoes or use it as a dip with veggies or pita bread.

12-ounce package soft silken tofu

1 cup peeled, seeded, and
chopped cucumber

1/4 cup lemon juice

1 clove garlic

2 teaspoons Dijon mustard

3/4 teaspoon dillweed

2 tablespoons extra-virgin olive
oil (optional)

Salt and pepper

In food processor, combine drained tofu, cucumber, lemon juice, garlic, mustard, and dillweed; purée until smooth. Add oil (if using), salt, and pepper and blend for 10 seconds. Store in refrigerator in covered container for up to 2 weeks.

GREENS DRESSING VARIATION: To 1 package tofu, add 1/4 cup chopped parsley, 1/4 cup cilantro, 2 tablespoons chopped fresh basil, 3–4 tablespoons lemon juice, 1 clove garlic, 1/2 teaspoon salt, and pinch pepper. Follow above directions.

Makes 2 1/2 cups

PER 2 TABLESPOONS: calories 12, protein: 1 g, carbohydrate: 1 g, fat: 0.6 g, dietary fiber: 0.1 g, sodium: 14 mg
WITH OIL: calories 24, fat: 2 g

% CALORIES FROM: protein 29%, fat 41%, carbohydrate, 30%
WITH OIL: % CALORIES FROM: protein 15%, fat 70%, carbohydrate 15%

Flaxseed and Tomato-Basil Dressing

 A tablespoon of this dressing will meet the generally accepted recommendations for omega-3 fatty acids for two days. This recipe was developed using Omega Nutrition's top quality flaxseed oil. The classic combination of garlic, basil, and tomatoes makes it a favorite to serve with salads such as Deep Green Leafy Salad or over steamed vegetables. It keeps well in the refrigerator.

1–2 tablespoons sun-dried tomatoes

1/4 cup apple cider vinegar

3–5 cloves garlic

3 tablespoons fresh basil (or 2 teaspoons dried)

1 teaspoon Dijon mustard

1 teaspoon tamari or soy sauce (optional)

1/2 teaspoon oregano

1/2 teaspoon tarragon

1/2 teaspoon maple syrup or other sweetener

6 drops Tabasco

3/4 cup flaxseed oil

Soak tomatoes in 1/4 cup hot water for 30 minutes or until soft. Drain. In blender or food processor, combine vinegar, garlic, basil, sun-dried tomatoes, mustard, tamari (if using), oregano, tarragon, sweetener, and Tabasco; blend until smooth. Slowly add oil in steady continuous stream.

Makes 1 cup

PER TABLESPOON: calories 100, protein: 0.2 g, carbohydrate: 0.6 g, fat: 10 g, dietary fiber: 0.1 g, sodium: 30 mg

EXCELLENT SOURCE OF: omega-3 fatty acids

% CALORIES FROM: protein 1%, fat 97%, carbohydrate 2 %

Lemon Tahini Dressing

 A delicious sesame seed butter, tahini can be used to flavor sauces and soups, or to give creamy texture to a dressing like this one. Flavors vary from brand to brand so look for one that appeals to you. Since tahini is not hydrogenated, oil may rise to its surface during storage; stir before using. The dressing keeps in the fridge for a week, so you may like this recipe enough to double it for use on baked potatoes another day!

1/3 cup plain soy milk or water

2 tablespoons lemon juice

1 teaspoon tamari or soy sauce

1 small clove garlic, chopped

1/4 teaspoon salt

Pinch pepper

1/4 cup tahini

Blend soy milk, lemon juice, tamari, garlic, salt, and pepper in blender or food processor. Add tahini and blend for 15 seconds or until smooth.

Makes 3/4 cup

PER TABLESPOON: calories 67, protein: 2 g, carbohydrate: 3 g, fat: 6 g, dietary fiber: 1 g, sodium: 153 mg

GOOD SOURCE OF: magnesium, thiamin

% CALORIES FROM: protein 12%, fat 73%, carbohydrate 15%

Orange Mint Dressing

 What a concept—a salad dressing without any oil! The mixture of mint and orange complements Apple Walnut Salad (page 88) and any salad of leafy greens and sprouts. Rice syrup is a very mild sweetener found in health food stores and Oriental markets.

1 cup frozen orange juice
  concentrate

1/2 cup water

1 tablespoon apple cider vinegar

1 teaspoon rice syrup or honey

1 teaspoon dried mint

1/2 teaspoon ground coriander

1/4 teaspoon salt

1/8 teaspoon pepper

Combine orange juice concentrate, water, vinegar, rice syrup, mint, coriander, salt, and pepper in a jar and shake until blended. Keep in refrigerator for up to 2 weeks.

Makes 1 1/3 cups

PER 2 TABLESPOONS: calories 43, protein: 1 g, carbohydrate: 10 g, fat: 0.1 g, dietary fiber: 0.2 g, sodium: 55 mg

EXCELLENT SOURCE OF: vitamin C
GOOD SOURCE OF: folate

% CALORIES FROM: protein 6%, fat 1%, carbohydrate 93%

Oriental Dressing

 Rice vinegar is a delicate vinegar with about half the acidity of other vinegars. The combination of rice vinegar and rice syrup with toasted sesame oil and the five spices in the Chinese seasoning— cinnamon, fennel, anise, star anise, and pepper—makes an intriguing blend in this favorite low-fat dressing developed by Vesanto. Serve with Calcium-Rich Greens on page 91 or use as a marinade for tofu.

1/4 cup rice vinegar

1/4 cup rice syrup or honey

1 tablespoon water

1 tablespoon canola oil

1 clove garlic, minced

1 teaspoon peeled, minced gingerroot

1/4 teaspoon toasted sesame oil

1/8 teaspoon Chinese 5-spice seasoning

In jar with lid, shake rice vinegar, rice syrup, water, oil, garlic, ginger, toasted sesame oil, and 5-spice seasoning for 15 seconds or until rice syrup is dissolved.

Makes 2/3 cup

PER TABLESPOON: calories 34, protein: 0, carbohydrate: 6 g, fat: 1 g, dietary fiber: 0, sodium: 9 mg

% CALORIES FROM: fat 34%, carbohydrate 66%

Raspberry Vinaigrette

 This dressing was designed as an enjoyable way for people to increase their intake of omega-3 fatty acids, using flaxseed oil. Since flaxseed oil may be strong tasting at first, use a mixture of flax and canola until you have acquired a taste. You may find that you enjoy this dressing on rice or baked potatoes, as well as many salad combinations.

1/2 cup flaxseed oil, canola oil, or mixture of both

3 tablespoons raspberry vinegar

2 tablespoons lemon juice

2 tablespoons tamari or soy sauce

2 tablespoons nutritional yeast (page 218)

1 teaspoon Dijon mustard

1/2 teaspoon finely minced garlic

Combine oil, vinegar, lemon juice, tamari, yeast, mustard, and garlic in a blender for 15 to 20 seconds.

Makes 1 cup

PER TABLESPOON: calories 64, protein: 0.4 g, carbohydrate: 0.6 g, fat: 7 g, dietary fiber: 0, sodium: 134 mg

EXCELLENT SOURCE OF: omega-3 fatty acids
GOOD SOURCE OF: thiamin

% CALORIES FROM: protein 2%, fat 94%, carbohydrate, 4%

Tofu Marinade

Tofu takes on other flavors very easily, hence its exceptional versatility. Here's a marinade that will make tofu seriously tasty. It can also be used to marinate tempeh for stir-fries or barbecues. It's also delicious as a light salad dressing or simply served over brown rice.

1/2 cup canned tomatoes	1 teaspoon chopped garlic
1/2 cup tamari or soy sauce	1 teaspoon minced, peeled
1/2 cup water	gingerroot
1/4 cup apple cider vinegar	1/2 teaspoon turmeric
2 tablespoons toasted sesame oil	

In blender, purée tomatoes, tamari, water, vinegar, sesame oil, garlic, ginger, and turmeric; blend for 10 seconds or until smooth. Cover bite-sized cubes of tofu or tempeh with marinade, and refrigerate for at least 4 hours. Transfer unused marinade to a jar with tight-fitting lid. This marinade keeps in refrigerator for 2 to 3 weeks.

Makes 1 3/4 cups

PER 2 TABLESPOONS: calories 13, protein: 0.5 g, carbohydrate: 1 g, fat: 2 g, dietary fiber: 0, sodium: 238 mg

% CALORIES FROM: protein 17%, fat 64%, carbohydrate 19%

Tofu Mayonnaise

 Here's an excellent and simple eggless mayo that you can make using firm silken tofu. Experiment with this basic recipe by adding a few capers, green onions, cilantro, garlic, or soaked sun-dried tomatoes to make your favorite mayo.

12-ounce package firm silken tofu

2 tablespoons lemon juice

2 tablespoons rice syrup or
   1 tablespoon honey

2 teaspoons rice vinegar

2 teaspoons extra-virgin olive oil
   (optional)

1 teaspoon prepared mustard

1 teaspoon nutritional yeast
   (page 218)

1/4 teaspoon salt

Pinch pepper

Drain tofu; place in food processor and blend for one minute, occasionally scraping down sides of bowl. Add lemon juice, rice syrup, vinegar, oil (if using), mustard, yeast, salt, and pepper; blend for 30 seconds until smooth. Store in covered container for up to 2 weeks.

Makes 1 2/3 cups

PER 2 TABLESPOONS: calories 25, protein: 2 g, carbohydrate: 3 g, fat: 0.9 g, dietary fiber: 0, sodium: 64 mg

% CALORIES FROM: protein 29%, fat 28%, carbohydrate 43%

Tomato-Herb Dressing

 This recipe can be varied according to your preferred herbs to create healthy, low-oil dressings. The tomato juice provides body and considerably reduces the amount of oil required. Try different herbs such as oregano or dill, on their own or in combination. If you use dried herbs instead of fresh, use one-third the amount specified for fresh herbs. You may also substitute apple cider vinegar for lemon juice or tomato-vegetable juice for tomato juice.

1 cup tomato juice	2 teaspoons chopped fresh basil
2 tablespoons lemon juice	1 teaspoon Dijon mustard
2 tablespoons apple cider vinegar	1/2 teaspoon dried tarragon
2 tablespoons flaxseed oil or	(optional)
extra-virgin olive oil or	Pinch pepper
mixture of both	

In jar with lid, combine tomato juice, lemon juice, vinegar, oil, basil, mustard, tarragon (if using), and pepper; shake for 30 seconds. Store in refrigerator for up to one week.

Makes 1 1/4 cups

PER 2 TABLESPOONS: calories 32, protein: 0.2 g, carbohydrate: 2 g, fat: 3 g, dietary fiber: 0.1 g, sodium: 100 mg (low-salt tomato juice will give a much lower sodium content)

EXCELLENT SOURCE OF: omega-3 fatty acids (with flaxseed oil)
GOOD SOURCE OF: vitamin C

% CALORIES FROM: protein 3%, fat 78%, carbohydrate 19%

Soups

Black Bean Soup

 Black beans are a tasty Mexican staple and can be used in salads, stews, and soups. The cumin and oregano give a southern accent to this soup. Adding lime juice just before serving adds a bright note.

4 cups vegetable stock

1 tablespoon canola oil (optional)

1 cup diced carrot

1 cup diced celery

1/2 onion, diced

1 clove garlic, minced

3 cups cooked black turtle beans
  or black beans

1/4 cup tomato paste

1 1/2 teaspoons ground cumin

1 teaspoon dried oregano

1 teaspoon dried thyme

2 teaspoons lime juice

Salt and pepper

Sauté carrots, celery, onions, and garlic in 2 tablespoons of the stock, adding more stock if necessary, or 1 tablespoon oil in large pot over medium heat for 5 minutes. Stir in beans, remaining stock, tomato paste, cumin, oregano, and thyme. Cover and simmer for 20 minutes or until vegetables are cooked. Just before serving, stir in lime juice. Stir in salt and pepper and adjust the seasoning.

Makes 4 servings, 1 1/2 cups each

PER SERVING: calories 251, protein: 13 g, carbohydrate: 51 g, fat: 1 g, dietary fiber: 11 g, sodium: 203 mg
WITH OIL: calories 262, fat 4 g

EXCELLENT SOURCE OF: iron, magnesium, potassium, folate, thiamin, vitamin A
GOOD SOURCE OF: calcium, zinc, vitamin B$_6$

% CALORIES FROM: protein 20%, fat 3%, carbohydrate 77%
WITH OIL: % CALORIES FROM: protein 19%, fat 15%, carbohydrate 66%

Carrot and Yam Soup

 Certain vitamins and phytochemicals in vegetables provide the splendid array of colors you see when you walk down the produce aisle. Three of these vitamins are bright yellow: riboflavin, folate, and vitamin A, also known as beta-carotene. This warming, golden soup is packed with all three!

4 cups vegetable stock

1 tablespoon canola oil (optional)

4 cups chopped carrots

2 cups peeled and chopped yam

1/2 small onion, sliced

1 1/2 teaspoons peeled, sliced gingerroot

1 cup apple juice

2 tablespoons orange juice concentrate

1 teaspoon ground coriander

1/4 teaspoon allspice

1/4 teaspoon nutmeg

1/4–1/2 teaspoon salt

Pinch pepper

Sauté carrots, yams, onion, and ginger in 2 tablespoons of the stock, adding more stock if necessary, or 1 tablespoon oil in large pot over medium heat for 3 to 5 minutes. Stir in remaining stock, apple juice, orange juice concentrate, coriander, allspice, nutmeg, salt, and pepper; reduce heat and simmer until carrots and yams are soft. Transfer to food processor or blender and purée until smooth. Return to pot to reheat and adjust seasoning.

Makes 4 servings

PER SERVING: calories 224, protein: 4 g, carbohydrate: 52 g, fat: 1 g, dietary fiber: 7 g, sodium: 392 mg
WITH OIL: calories 254, fat: 4 g

EXCELLENT SOURCE OF: potassium, vitamins A, B6, and C
GOOD SOURCE OF: iron, magnesium, folate, riboflavin, thiamin

% CALORIES FROM: protein 7%, fat 3%, carbohydrate 90%
WITH OIL: % CALORIES FROM: protein 6%, fat 14%, carbohydrate 80%

Creamy Vegetable Soup

 Tahini makes this hearty soup extra creamy. Broccoli, kale, and Chinese cabbage have become favorites of many people because the calcium in these greens is highly available to the body. This soup also provides iron, magnesium, potassium, and zinc, and is packed with vitamins!

6 1/2 cups water

1/2 cup brown rice

1 clove garlic, minced

1 teaspoon peeled, minced
   gingerroot

1 cup diced carrots

1 cup diced zucchini

1 cup sliced broccoli

1 cup sliced Chinese cabbage

1 cup sliced kale

1/3 cup tahini

2 tablespoons tamari or
   soy sauce

2 tablespoons miso (optional)

1 tablespoon diced green onion

In a covered pot, combine water, rice, garlic, and ginger; simmer for 45 minutes. Add carrots; cook for 5 minutes. Add zucchini, broccoli, cabbage, and kale; cook for 5 more minutes. In small bowl, combine tahini, tamari, and miso along with 1/2 cup of liquid from soup; mix into smooth paste. Add to soup. Adjust seasoning and garnish with green onions.

Makes 4 servings

PER SERVING: Calories 254, protein: 9 g, carbohydrate: 31 g, fat: 12 g, dietary fiber: 6 g, sodium: 568 mg

EXCELLENT SOURCE OF: magnesium, zinc, thiamin, vitamins A, B_6, and C
GOOD SOURCE OF: calcium, iron, potassium, folate, niacin, omega-3 fatty acids

% CALORIES FROM: protein 13%, fat 41%, carbohydrate 46%

Lentil Soup

 Adapted from the Moosewood Cookbook, *by Mollie Katzen (Ten Speed Press), this recipe takes considerably less time than the original; however, the taste is still spectacular. Thank you, Mollie!*

4 cups vegetable stock

1 tablespoon canola oil (optional)

1/2 onion, chopped

1 large clove garlic, minced

2 cups fresh or canned tomatoes, chopped

1 cup dried lentils

1 teaspoon dried oregano

1 teaspoon dried basil

2 bay leaves

1 cup diced carrots

1 cup diced celery

2 tablespoons blackstrap molasses or brown sugar

1 tablespoon apple cider vinegar

1/4–1/2 teaspoon salt

1/8 teaspoon pepper

Sauté onion and garlic in 2 tablespoons stock, adding more stock if necessary, or 1 tablespoon oil in large pot over medium heat for 5 minutes. Stir in remaining stock, tomatoes, lentils, oregano, basil, and bay leaves. Cover and simmer for 45 minutes. Add carrots, celery, molasses, vinegar, salt, and pepper; cook for 12 to 15 minutes or until vegetables are tender-crisp. Remove bay leaves. Adjust seasoning.

Makes 4 servings

PER SERVING: calories 241, protein: 15 g, carbohydrate: 46 g, fat: 1 g, dietary fiber: 18 g, sodium: 232 mg

EXCELLENT SOURCE OF: iron, magnesium, potassium, folate, thiamin, vitamins A, B6, and C
GOOD SOURCE OF: calcium, zinc, niacin, riboflavin

% CALORIES FROM: protein 24%, fat 4%, carbohydrate 72%

Minestrone Soup

While working in the banquet kitchen at the Four Season's Hotel in Vancouver, Joseph used to make animal-based soup stocks using hundreds of pounds of animal bones. He would regularly make soups in 100-quart batches. This recipe calls for vegetable stock, serves only four, and has a no-oil option. Enjoy!

4 cups vegetable stock (recipe page 125)

1 tablespoon olive oil (optional)

1 cup diced carrots

1 cup diced celery

1/2 large onion, diced

2 cloves garlic, minced

1 cup diced potato

2 cups chopped fresh or canned tomatoes

2 tablespoons tomato paste

1 teaspoon dried basil

1/2 teaspoon dried oregano

1/4 teaspoon celery seeds

1/4–1/2 teaspoon salt

Pinch pepper

1 cup sliced zucchini

1 cup sliced green or yellow beans

1/2 cup cooked garbanzo, kidney, or white beans

2 tablespoons chopped parsley

Sauté carrots, celery, onions, and garlic in 2 tablespoons of the stock, adding more stock if necessary, or 1 tablespoon oil in large pot over medium heat for 5 minutes. Stir in remaining stock, potatoes, tomatoes, tomato paste, basil, oregano, celery seeds, salt, and pepper. Cover, reduce heat, and simmer for about 20 minutes. Add zucchini, green beans, and your choice of legumes. Cover and cook for about 5 to 7 minutes or until potatoes are cooked and vegetables are tender-crisp. Adjust seasoning and garnish with parsley.

Makes 4 servings

PER SERVING: calories 163, protein: 6 g, carbohydrate: 35 g, fat: 1 g, dietary fiber: 8 g, sodium: 298 mg
WITH OIL: calories 193, fat: 5 g

EXCELLENT SOURCE OF: potassium, folate, vitamins A, B$_6$, and C
GOOD SOURCE OF: calcium, iron, magnesium, niacin, riboflavin, thiamin

% CALORIES FROM: protein 14%, fat 8%, carbohydrate 78%
WITH OIL: % CALORIES FROM: protein 12%, fat 21%, carbohydrate 67%

Miso Ginger Soup

 Miso is a rich, thick fermented soybean paste from Japan, where it is credited with many healthful qualities. Depending on the grain used in combination with soybeans and the length of fermentation, each miso has its own distinct aroma, flavor, color, and use. Lighter miso is sweeter and better for summer use while darker miso is more robust and suited to the colder months. Mirin is a seasoned Japanese cooking wine.

4 1/2 cups water

1/4 cup thinly sliced gingerroot
   (unpeeled)

1 small clove garlic, chopped

1/2 cup diagonally sliced carrot

1/2 cup thinly sliced napa cabbage

1/4 cup snow peas

1/3 cup miso

2 tablespoons mirin

1/4 cup finely diced firm tofu

2 tablespoons chopped green
   onion

Bring water, ginger, and garlic to a boil in large pot. Reduce heat and simmer over medium heat for 10 minutes. Strain liquid, discarding ginger and garlic, then return liquid to pot. Bring stock to boil. Add carrots; reduce heat and simmer for 5 minutes. Add cabbage and snow peas; simmer for 2 to 3 minutes. Combine miso, mirin, and 1 cup of stock in small bowl, mixing with fork until miso is dissolved. Remove pot from heat. Stir in miso mixture; add tofu and green onion. Return to heat, but do not boil.

Makes 4 servings

PER SERVING: calories 105, protein: 6 g, carbohydrate: 13 g, fat: 3 g, dietary fiber: 3 g, sodium: 861 mg, alcohol: 1 g

EXCELLENT SOURCE OF: vitamin A
GOOD SOURCE OF: calcium, iron, vitamin C, omega-3 fatty acids

% CALORIES FROM: protein 22%, fat 23%, carbohydrate 49%, alcohol (in mirin) 6%

Mulligatawny Soup

 In one of the languages of Southern India, mulligatawny *means "pepper water." The spiciness varies according to how much pepper and ginger you add, so if you like it hot, add more, as this version is mild. The sweetness of apple and celery balances the spice.*

4 cups vegetable stock

1 tablespoon canola oil (optional)

1 cup sliced celery

1 apple, diced

1/2 onion, diced

1 teaspoon peeled, minced
  gingerroot

1 clove garlic, minced

1 tablespoon tomato paste

1 1/2 teaspoons curry powder

1/4 teaspoon celery seeds

1/4 teaspoon salt

1/8–1/4 teaspoon black pepper

1/4 cup white basmati rice

Sauté celery, apple, onion, ginger, and garlic in 2 tablespoons of the stock, adding more stock if necessary, or 1 tablespoon oil in large pot over medium heat for 5 minutes. Stir in tomato paste, curry powder, celery seeds, salt, and pepper. Cook for 5 minutes, stirring frequently to prevent sticking. Add remaining stock and basmati rice. Bring to boil. Cover, reduce heat, and simmer for 30 minutes, stirring occasionally. Adjust seasoning.

Makes 3–4 servings

PER SERVING: calories 117, protein: 3 g, carbohydrate: 27 g, fat: 0.7 g, dietary fiber: 3 g, sodium: 294 mg
WITH OIL: calories 111, fat 4 g

% CALORIES FROM: protein 8%, fat 5%, carbohydrate 87%
WITH OIL: % CALORIES FROM: protein 6%, fat 29%, carbohydrate 65%

Mushroom Broth

 With the variety of mushrooms on the market today—regular field, crimini, oyster, shitake, and Portobello—this light soup can have a number of variations. Marjoram and thyme complement mushrooms by accentuating their flavor. Vegetable stock is essential in this recipe; dissolve vegetable bouillon cubes or powder in boiling water or make your own from scratch (page 125). If using cubes, choose those without hydrogenated fats (such as Organic Gourmet).

6 cups vegetable stock	1/2 teaspoon dried marjoram
1 tablespoon canola oil (optional)	1/4 teaspoon dried thyme
4 cups thinly sliced fresh mushrooms	1/4 teaspoon salt
	1/8 teaspoon pepper
4 green onions, chopped	1 tablespoon chopped parsley

Sauté mushrooms in 2 tablespoons of the stock, adding more stock if necessary, or in 1 tablespoon oil in large pot over medium heat for 5 minutes or until they start to brown. Add remaining stock, green onions, marjoram, thyme, salt, and pepper; simmer for 10 minutes. Adjust seasoning. Divide broth among 4 serving bowls. Garnish with parsley.

Makes 4 servings

PER SERVING: calories 23, protein: 2 g, carbohydrate: 4 g, fat: 0.4 g, dietary fiber: 0.2 g, sodium: 160 mg
WITH OIL: calories 53, fat: 4 g

GOOD SOURCE OF: riboflavin, niacin, vitamin D

% CALORIES FROM: protein 26%, fat 12%, carbohydrate 62%
WITH OIL: % CALORIES FROM: protein 12%, fat 59%, carbohydrate 29%

Spicy Eggplant Soup

This soup makes a warming and aromatic meal, accompanied by a slice of bread with Morroc-Un-Butter, page 79. For added spiciness increase the ginger or pepper to taste.

7 cups vegetable stock

1 tablespoon olive oil (optional)

2 carrots, diced

2 potatoes, diced

1 onion, diced

1 eggplant, cubed

2 tablespoons grated gingerroot

2 cloves garlic, minced

1 cup chopped fresh or canned tomatoes

1/2 cup chopped fresh cilantro

1 teaspoon cumin

1/2 teaspoon pepper

Salt

In large pot, sauté carrots, potatoes, onion, eggplant, ginger, and garlic over medium heat in 2 tablespoons stock, adding more stock if necessary, or in 1 tablespoon oil for 3 to 5 minutes or until onions are soft. Stir in remaining stock, tomatoes, cilantro, cumin, and pepper; cover, bring to boil, then lower heat and simmer for 20 to 30 minutes or until potatoes are cooked. Adjust seasoning.

Makes 6 servings

PER SERVING: calories 94, protein: 3 g, carbohydrate: 22 g, fat: 0.5 g, dietary fiber: 5 g, sodium: 82 mg
WITH OIL: calories 114, fat: 3 g

EXCELLENT SOURCE OF: vitamin A
GOOD SOURCE OF: potassium, thiamin, vitamins B_6 and C

% CALORIES FROM: protein 10%, fat 4%, carbohydrate 86%
WITH OIL: % CALORIES FROM: protein 9%, fat 20%, carbohydrate 71%

Split Pea Soup with Veggie Back Bacon

Yves Potvin of Yves Veggie Cuisine has developed a number of completely plant-based meat analogues that are exceptional in quality. His Veggie Back Bacon has a delicate smoked flavor that adds a wonderful base note to this recipe. Served with a wholesome bread and salad, this soup easily satisfies the heartiest appetites.

8 cups vegetable stock	3 bay leaves
1 tablespoon canola oil (optional)	5 whole cloves
1 cup diced carrot	1/4–1/2 teaspoon salt
1 cup diced celery	1/8 teaspoon black pepper
1/2 onion, diced	3 slices Yves Veggie Back Bacon,
2 cloves garlic, minced	diced small
2 cups dried green split peas,	1 tablespoon chopped fresh
rinsed	parsley

Sauté carrots, celery, onions, and garlic in 2 tablespoons of the stock, adding more stock if necessary, or in 1 tablespoon oil in large pot over medium heat for 5 minutes. Stir in remaining stock, split peas, bay leaves, and cloves. Bring to boil, cover, reduce heat, and simmer for 45 to 60 minutes. Add salt, pepper, Veggie Back Bacon and more liquid if soup is too thick. Remove bay leaves before serving. Adjust seasoning. Garnish with parsley.

Makes 4–5 servings

PER SERVING (1/4 RECIPE): calories 393, protein: 26 g, carbohydrate: 69 g, fat: 1 g, dietary fiber: 28 g, sodium: 313 mg
WITH OIL: calories 423, fat 5 g

EXCELLENT SOURCE OF: iron, magnesium, potassium, zinc, folate, thiamin, vitamin A
GOOD SOURCE OF: calcium, niacin, riboflavin, vitamin B6

% CALORIES FROM: protein 26%, fat 3%, carbohydrate 71%
WITH OIL: % CALORIES FROM: protein 24%, fat 10%, carbohydrate 66%

Vegetable Noodle Soup

 Freshly crushed coriander seeds give this soup a unique twist. Its pleasant aromatic taste suggests a mixture of caraway and cumin. Combined here with carrots and yams, a sweetness comes through that is subtle and nourishing.

1/2 cup uncooked spiral, shell, or elbow noodles

4 cups vegetable stock

1 tablespoon canola oil (optional)

1/2 cup diced carrot

1/2 cup diced celery

1/2 cup diced turnip

1/2 cup diced yam

1/2 onion, diced

1 clove garlic, minced

2 tablespoons chopped fresh parsley

1 teaspoon crushed coriander seeds

1/4–1/2 teaspoon salt

Pinch pepper

Cook noodles according to package directions and set aside. Sauté carrot, celery, turnip, yam, onion, and garlic in 2 tablespoons of the stock, adding more stock if necessary, or in 1 tablespoon canola oil in large pot over medium heat for 5 minutes. Add remaining stock, parsley, and coriander seeds; cover, and simmer for 15 minutes or until vegetables are tender-crisp. Add noodles, salt and pepper. Adjust seasoning.

Makes 4 cups

PER SERVING: calories 114, protein: 3 g, carbohydrate: 25 g, fat: 0.5 g, dietary fiber: 1 g, sodium: 200 mg
WITH OIL: calories 144, fat: 4 g

EXCELLENT SOURCE OF: vitamin A
GOOD SOURCE OF: vitamin B6

% CALORIES FROM: protein 12%, fat 4%, carbohydrate 83%
WITH OIL: % CALORIES FROM: protein 8%, fat 24%, carbohydrate 68%

Vegetable Stock

 This simple stock can be kept on hand in the refrigerator for 4 to 5 days or made in larger quantities and frozen. The no-oil method of cooking, featured in many recipes and explained in detail on page 48, calls for the use of 2 tablespoons of stock or more if necessary. Each compartment of an ice cube tray will hold 2 tablespoons of stock, thereby facilitating the storage of frozen stock cubes for this method of cooking. Once frozen, remove stock cubes from the tray and store in a heavy plastic bag as ice cubes left exposed in the freezer will shrink due to evaporation. When making stock from scratch, try substituting different vegetables such as tomatoes, fennel, leeks, and mushrooms, or herbs, such as basil, rosemary, and coriander. Avoid cabbage family vegetables in your stock as their taste and odor are overpowering. If using commercial stock cubes, choose one that does not contain MSG or hydrogenated fats.

6 cups water	2 large cloves garlic, chopped
2 carrots, diced	1/2 teaspoon dried thyme
2 stalks celery, diced	10 peppercorns, crushed
1 large onion, chopped	3 bay leaves
1/4 cup parsley leaves and stems	3 whole cloves

Place water, carrots, celery, onion, parsley, garlic, thyme, peppercorns, bay leaves, and cloves in large pot; bring to simmer and cook, uncovered, for 30 minutes. Strain through colander or sieve. Discard vegetables and let stock cool before refrigerating or freezing.

Makes 6 cups

Entrées

African Stew

 Peanut butter makes a wonderful, creamy sauce for this nutrition-packed stew that is likely to become a family favorite. Lemon juice added at the end gives a lively nuance to the flavor. Season with a dash of hot pepper sauce, fiery chipotle sauce, or Vietnamese chili sauce.

4 cups vegetable stock

1 onion, chopped

2 cloves garlic, minced

2 cups peeled diced yams

1 cup cooked chick-peas

1/2 cup brown rice

1/4 teaspoon salt

1/4 cup peanut butter

2 cups chopped kale

2 tablespoons lemon juice

Tamari or soy sauce (optional)

Chili sauce

Sauté onions and garlic in 2 tablespoons of the stock, adding more stock if necessary, or in 1 tablespoon oil in large pot over medium heat for 5 minutes. Add remaining stock, yams, chick-peas, rice, and salt; simmer for 45 minutes. In small bowl, blend peanut butter and 1/2 cup of liquid from stew to make a smooth paste. Stir into stew along with kale and cook for 5 minutes. Stir in lemon juice and tamari (if using). Add chili sauce to taste. Adjust seasoning.

Makes 4 servings

PER SERVING: calories 451, protein: 14 g, carbohydrate: 79 g, fat: 11g, dietary fiber: 10 g, sodium: 169 mg

EXCELLENT SOURCE OF: magnesium, potassium, folate, niacin, riboflavin, thiamin vitamins A, B$_6$, and C
GOOD SOURCE OF: calcium, iron, zinc, vitamin E

% CALORIES FROM: protein 12%, fat 20%, carbohydrate 68%

Ross Durant

Ross Durant

Ross Durant

Fruit Shakes PAGE 62

photo courtesy of the B.C. Blueberry Council

Ross Durant

Cashew Cheese Lasagna

Cashews provide a wonderful cheesy-tasting topping for this very tasty lasagna. Salt is added during the processing of canned tomato products, so if you're trying to lower your sodium intake, try one of the low-sodium sauces available on the market. The lemon juice called for in the topping is best fresh, however, frozen pure lemon juice will also work.

Cashew Cheese

1 1/2 cups raw, unsalted cashew pieces	1/3 cup lemon juice
1 1/2 cups water	4 teaspoons tamari or soy sauce
1/3 cup nutritional yeast (page 218)	2 teaspoons onion powder
	1 teaspoon celery seed
	1/2 teaspoon garlic powder

Blend cashews, water, yeast, lemon juice, tamari, onion powder, celery seed, and garlic powder in blender for 1 minute or until very smooth.

Lasagna

6 lasagna noodles	1/2 onion, diced
2 12-ounce packages extra-firm silken tofu	1/2 teaspoon dried basil
2 tablespoons vegetable stock or water	1/2 teaspoon oregano
2 cups chopped mushrooms	1/2 teaspoon salt
1 cup diced celery	1/8 teaspoon pepper
	1 1/2 cups tomato sauce
	1 large tomato, sliced

Cook noodles according to package directions. Drain and cool under cold running water. Meanwhile mash tofu in large bowl. In skillet over medium heat, sauté mushrooms, celery, and onion in stock for 5 minutes, adding more stock if necessary. Transfer to bowl with tofu along with basil, oregano, salt, and pepper, stirring to mix.

{continued}

To assemble

Preheat oven to 350°. Spread 1/3 cup of tomato sauce on bottom of 9 x 13-inch baking dish. Lay 3 noodles over sauce. Spoon half of tofu mix over noodles, followed by remaining tomato sauce, noodles, and tofu mixture. Pour cashew cheese as final layer and spread evenly over filling. Top with tomato slices and bake for 30 to 40 minutes or until cashew cheese has set and moisture bubbles along the sides of pan.

Makes 8 servings

PER SERVING: calories 310, protein: 17 g, carbohydrate: 33 g, fat: 15 g, dietary fiber: 3 g, sodium: 536 mg

EXCELLENT SOURCE OF: iron, magnesium, zinc, folate, niacin, riboflavin, thiamin, vitamins B_6 and B_{12}
GOOD SOURCE OF: potassium

% CALORIES FROM: protein 20%, fat 40%, carbohydrate 40%

Chili with Textured Soy Protein

 When iron-rich foods such as kidney beans or textured soy protein are eaten with vitamin C-rich foods such as tomatoes, onions, and peppers, the body's absorption of iron is greatly increased.

2 cups vegetable stock

1 cup diced carrots

1 cup diced celery

1 cup diced green peppers

1/2 onion, diced

2 cloves garlic, minced

1 tablespoon canola oil (optional)

2 cups cooked or canned kidney beans, drained

2 cups chopped fresh or canned tomatoes

1/4 cup tomato paste

1/2 cup textured soy protein

1 teaspoon ground cumin

1 teaspoon dried basil

1 teaspoon chili powder

1/4 teaspoon black pepper

2 bay leaves

Salt

2 tablespoons chopped fresh cilantro

Sauté carrots, celery, green peppers, onions, and garlic in 2 tablespoons of the stock, adding more stock if necessary, or in 1 tablespoon oil in large pot over medium heat for 5 minutes or until onions are soft. Stir in remaining stock, beans, tomatoes, tomato paste, textured soy protein, cumin, basil, chili powder, pepper, and bay leaves. Bring to boil then reduce heat, cover, and simmer 20 minutes. Adjust seasoning, remove bay leaves, and garnish with cilantro.

VARIATION: Textured soy protein may be replaced with uncooked medium-grade bulgur.

Makes 4 servings

PER SERVING: calories 236, protein: 17 g, carbohydrate: 45 g, fat: 2 g, dietary fiber: 14 g, sodium: 218 mg*   WITH OIL: calories: 267, fat: 5 g

EXCELLENT SOURCE OF: iron, magnesium, potassium, folate, thiamin, vitamins A, B6, and C
GOOD SOURCE OF: calcium, zinc, niacin, riboflavin

% CALORIES FROM: protein 26%, fat 5%, carbohydrate 69%
WITH OIL: % CALORIES FROM: protein 23%, fat 16%, carbohydrate 61%

*Sodium will be higher with canned tomatoes.

Crispy Tofu Fingers

 If you want to introduce tofu to your family or friends, this is one of the best ways we've ever found to prepare it. The seasoning salt called Spike, regular or unsalted, is available at supermarkets. Pan-fried, the tofu takes on a crispy southern-fried taste. As a lower-fat option, these may be baked. Some people like tofu moist, and others like it dry, so experiment a little with the cooking time. Crispy Tofu can be used as the protein part of a dinner, as an appetizer, as a topping for pizza, or in sandwiches.

12-ounce package extra-firm tofu

1–2 tablespoons light or regular tamari or soy sauce

1/4 cup nutritional yeast (page 218)

1 teaspoon Spike or other dehydrated vegetable seasoning

1 tablespoon canola oil (if frying)

Cut tofu into 1/4-inch slices. Pour tamari into flat-bottomed bowl. In another bowl, combine yeast with Spike. Dip tofu slices into tamari, then into yeast mixture to coat both sides. Pan-fry coated tofu in a little oil over medium heat for 2 to 3 minutes or until crispy brown. Turn and repeat.

Alternatively, place prepared tofu on a lightly oiled or nonstick baking sheet and bake at 350° for about 15 minutes, or until tofu just begins to brown.

Makes 3 servings

PER SERVING: calories 189, protein: 22 g, carbohydrate: 7 g, fat: 10 g, dietary fiber: 3 g, sodium: 532 mg
WITH OIL: calories 229, fat 15 g

EXCELLENT SOURCE OF: calcium*, iron, magnesium, zinc, folate, niacin, riboflavin, thiamin, vitamins B_6 and B_{12}*, omega-3 fatty acids
GOOD SOURCE OF: magnesium, potassium

% CALORIES FROM: protein 42%, fat 44%, carbohydrate 14%
WITH OIL: % CALORIES FROM: protein 35%, fat 53%, carbohydrate 12%

*Analyzed using Red Star Vegetarian Support Formula Nutritional Yeast, light soy sauce, and tofu set with calcium.

Curried Vegetables with Tofu

Here is a rich dish with a coconut milk-based sauce to enjoy from time to time, and a concentrated source of calories for those with high-energy needs. It is designed to be served with basmati rice. For a change, make this curry without tofu and serve it with East Indian Chick-Peas (page 137). The crispy crackers called papadums (see next page) are a great addition any time East Indian dishes are served.

1/4 cup raisins

1 onion, diced

1 clove garlic, minced

1 teaspoon peeled, minced
  gingerroot

1 tablespoon canola oil

1 teaspoon curry powder

1 teaspoon cumin

1/2 teaspoon coriander

1/2 teaspoon turmeric

1/2 teaspoon salt

1 cup diced carrots

1 cup diced red bell pepper

1 cup broccoli florets

1 cup cauliflower florets

1 cup firm tofu, diced

7 ounces coconut milk

2 teaspoons lime juice

1 tablespoon chopped fresh
  cilantro

1/4 cup unsalted cashews
  (optional)

Cover raisins with boiling water and soak for 15 to 20 minutes. Sauté onion, garlic, and ginger in oil over medium heat for 5 minutes. Stir in curry, cumin, coriander, turmeric, and salt; sauté for 5 minutes. Strain raisins and add to pan along with carrots, red pepper, broccoli, cauliflower, tofu, and coconut milk; simmer until vegetables are tender and crisp. Stir in lime juice, cilantro, and cashews (if using).

Makes 4 servings

PER SERVING: calories 468, protein: 22 g, carbohydrate: 38 g, fat: 30 g, dietary fiber: 10 g, sodium: 526 mg

EXCELLENT SOURCE OF: calcium, iron, magnesium, potassium, folate, thiamin, vitamins A, B6, and C
GOOD SOURCE OF: zinc, niacin, riboflavin

% CALORIES FROM: protein 17%, fat 53%, carbohydrate 30%

Papadums

Papadums are crispy, paper-thin crackers made with chick-pea flour and spices and are available at East Indian grocery stores. They can be mild or spicy depending on the type and amount of seasonings used. They can be eaten as an appetizer with chutney or as an accompaniment to a curry dinner. Though often deep fried when served in a restaurant, they have no added fat when prepared under a broiler.

To prepare them the no-fat way, preheat broiler and place oven rack 6 inches below broiler. Place 2 papadums on rack and broil, watching carefully. Once heat begins to blister papadum, move it around using tongs, until heat blisters every part of cracker (about 20 to 30 seconds). Turn papadum over. Remove from oven once papadum is completely blistered on both sides. Papadums may also be heated for 45 seconds on high in a microwave oven.

Curry in a Hurry

Good quality curry paste brings the rich spices of the East directly into your kitchen, allowing you to produce a tasty curry in minutes. Red lentils are the fastest-cooking legume; by serving them with white basmati rice, you can produce a nourishing meal in less than 30 minutes. You may want to add leftover cooked vegetables such as carrots, cauliflower, or zucchini in the last 5 minutes of cooking.

2 tablespoons vegetable stock
  or water
1 cup chopped tomato
1/2 onion, diced
1 clove garlic, minced

1 tablespoon mild curry paste
2 1/2 cups water
1 cup dried red lentils
1/4 teaspoon salt

Sauté tomato, onion, garlic, and curry paste in 2 tablespoons stock or water in pot over medium heat for 3 to 5 minutes. Stir in water and lentils. Cover and simmer for 20 minutes. Add salt and adjust seasoning.

VARIATION: When you can allow more cooking time, make this dish using the slower cooking green, brown, or gray lentils, simmering the curry for 45 minutes instead of 20 minutes. These lentils are higher in the minerals iron, magnesium, potassium, and zinc and the vitamins folate and thiamin than are the red lentils.

Makes 4 servings

PER SERVING: calories 185, protein: 12 g, carbohydrate: 32 g, fat: 2 g, dietary fiber: 8 g, sodium: 170 mg

GOOD SOURCE OF: iron, thiamin

% CALORIES FROM: protein 25%, fat 9%, carbohydrate 66%

Delicious Sandwiches, Vegetarian Style

 Go to the bakery and choose multigrain breads for tomorrow's lunch, or if you're a bread-making enthusiast, bake your own. Here are some great combinations:

- Crispy Tofu Fingers (page 132), tomato slices, lettuce, mayo
- Almond, cashew, or peanut butter or tahini; jam, rice syrup or honey; sliced banana
- Avocado Dip (page 72), sweet red bell peppers
- Black Bean Hummus (page 73), tomato or cucumber slices, avocado slices
- Curry Sandwich Spread (page 74), lettuce
- Gee Whiz Spread (page 75), cucumber slices
- Gooda Cheeze (page 77), alfalfa sprouts, mayo
- Hummus (page 78), tomato or cucumber slices, chopped olives
- warmed Marinated Tofu (page 110), alfalfa sprouts
- Pesto-the Best-Oh! (page 80), canned artichoke slices
- Veggieburger or tofuburger (heated), red onion slice, tomato, ketchup, relish, mustard, sprouts

The following are particularly low in fat:

- Yves Veggie Pepperoni or Deli Slices, dill pickle slices, tomato slices, Dijon mustard, Tofu Mayonnaise (page 111)
- Baked Eggplant (page 164); tomato slices, green pepper slices
- Roasted Garlic and Yam Spread (page 82)
- Black Bean Hummus (page 73) or the low-fat variation of Hummus (page 78), tomato or cucumber slices

These are other sandwiches from other parts of the world:

- Vegetarian Sushi Rolls (page 150 or from a Japanese restaurant or deli), tamari or soy sauce, wasabi, pickled ginger
- Salad Roll (page 95), Spicy Peanut Sauce (page 190), Teriyaki Sauce (page 192), barbecue or plum sauce
- International Roll-Ups (page 139)

East Indian Chick-Peas

 Once you've discovered curry pastes, you'll enjoy the ease with which you can put together a vegetable or bean curry. Even the mild pastes are hot enough for most people. The Patak brand is our favorite. Use a little or a lot, depending on your preference. Chick-peas are high in trace minerals and the vitamin folate.

2 cups chopped fresh or canned tomatoes

1 onion, diced

2 cloves garlic, minced

1 tablespoon canola oil (optional)

1–3 teaspoons mild curry paste

3 cups cooked chick-peas

1 tablespoon lemon juice

1 teaspoon tamari or soy sauce

1/4 teaspoon salt (optional)

Sauté tomatoes, onions, and garlic in 2 tablespoons stock or water, adding more if necessary, or in 1 tablespoon oil in skillet over medium heat for 3 to 5 minutes, until onions are soft. Stir in curry paste and cook for 3 minutes. Add chick-peas, lemon juice, and tamari; cook for 15 minutes. Season to taste.

Makes 4 servings

PER SERVING: calories 248, protein: 12 g, carbohydrate: 43 g, fat: 4 g, dietary fiber: 11 g, sodium: 271 mg
WITH OIL: calories 278, fat 7 g

EXCELLENT SOURCE OF: iron, magnesium potassium, folate, vitamin C
GOOD SOURCE OF: calcium, zinc, thiamin, vitamin B6

% CALORIES FROM: protein 19%, fat 15%, carbohydrate 66%
WITH OIL: % CALORIES FROM: protein 16%, fat 24%, carbohydrate 60%

Figs and Beans
Faba in Frixorio (Beans in the Frying Pan)

 Who would have thought of combining figs, kidney beans, and herbs? In fact, this dish was prepared by the famed 16th-century vegetarian Leonardo da Vinci (probably known to his friends as Leonardo da Veggie). In his delightful book Famous Vegetarians and Their Favorite Recipes, *Rynn Berry describes this dish, as well as favorites from the days of Pythagoras, Plato, and Socrates and up to modern times. The original instructions read: "In a greased frying pan combine cooked beans with onions, chopped figs, sage, garlic and various kitchen herbs. Fry well in oil. Sprinkle with aromatic herbs and serve."*

1 cup dried figs	1/4 teaspoon thyme
1 onion, chopped	1/4 teaspoon rosemary
1 clove garlic, minced	Pinch dried sage
1 tablespoon olive oil	Salt and pepper
3 cups cooked kidney beans, drained	2 tablespoons chopped fresh parsley
1/4 teaspoon dried basil	

Soak figs in water for 12 hours. Reserve soaking liquid. Remove stems from figs; chop and set aside. Sauté onion and garlic in oil over medium heat for 5 minutes or until onions are soft. Add beans, figs, 1/2 cup of soaking liquid, basil, thyme, rosemary, and sage; cook on low heat for 10 minutes or until beans are heated through. Season to taste and stir in parsley.

Makes 4 servings

PER SERVING: calories 339, protein: 14 g, carbohydrate: 66 g, fat: 5 g, dietary fiber: 14 g, sodium: 10 mg

EXCELLENT SOURCE OF: iron, magnesium, potassium, folate
GOOD SOURCE OF: calcium, zinc, thiamin, vitamins B$_6$ and E

% CALORIES FROM: protein 15%, fat 12%, carbohydrate 73%

International Roll-Ups

The basic roll-up begins with a 9-inch tortilla. It is a fabulous way of introducing exotic flavors into your menus. These roll-ups are packed with nutrition and easy to make and they provide an opportunity to use leftovers. After trying a few variations, you'll discover your own favorite flavor combinations and before you know it, you'll be globe-traveling on your lunch break. Gather and prepare all ingredients and lay them out on the counter. To assemble, spread a strip of rice on tortilla, followed by vegetables and sauce. Lift edge of tortilla and roll snugly.

African-Style

1/3 cup cooked brown rice
1/3 cup cooked mashed yam
1/3 cup sliced kale, lightly
   steamed

2 tablespoons Spicy Peanut Sauce
   (page 190)
1/4 cup alfalfa sprouts
Dash hot pepper sauce (optional)

Indonesian-Style

1/2 cup cooked brown rice
2 ounces Lemon Ginger Tempeh
   (page 141)
1/4 cup sliced napa cabbage
2 tablespoons sliced water
   chestnuts

1 teaspoon thinly sliced pickled
   gingerroot
2 teaspoons Tamarind Date Sauce
   (page 191)

Italian-Style

1/2 cup cooked brown rice
1/2 cup raw spinach, steamed
2 artichoke hearts, sliced

1 teaspoon chopped fresh basil
1 lettuce leaf
2 tablespoons tomato sauce

Mexican-Style

1/2 cup cooked brown rice
1/4 cup grated carrot
1/4 cup shredded soy cheese
  or cheddar
1 teaspoon chopped fresh cilantro

2 teaspoons mayonnaise (Tofu,
  page 111, or commercial)
1 lettuce leaf, cut into strips
2 teaspoons salsa

Middle Eastern-Style

1/2 cup Hummus (page 78)
1/4 cup chopped fresh tomato
1/4 cup grated carrot
1 tablespoon chopped fresh
  parsley

1 lettuce leaf
2 tablespoons Lemon Tahini
  Dressing (page 106)

Japanese-Style

1/2 cup cooked brown rice
1/4 cup grated carrot
1/4 cup grated daikon radish
2 teaspoons mayonnaise
  (Tofu, page 111, or commercial)
2 teaspoons thinly sliced pickled
  gingerroot

1/2 teaspoon Gomasio (optional,
  page 76 or commercial)
1 tablespoon thinly sliced green
  onion
2 teaspoons Teriyaki Sauce
  (page 192)

FOR 1 JAPANESE ROLL-UP: calories 231, protein: 17 g, carbohydrate: 52 g, fat: 2 g, dietary fiber: 5 g, sodium: 295 mg

EXCELLENT SOURCE OF: magnesium, vitamins A and C
GOOD SOURCE OF: iron, potassium, niacin, thiamin, vitamin B6

% CALORIES FROM: protein 11%, fat 6%, carbohydrate 82%

Lasagna Al Forno

A new and improved version of an old standard, this savory lasagna has a filling made with tofu and is topped with soy cheese. Serve it with the crunchy Caesar Salad (page 90) and a crusty loaf of bread for a satisfying meal for your family and guests.

12 ounces extra-firm tofu, crumbled

2 bunches spinach, washed, cooked, drained, and chopped

1 cup grated soy cheese or dairy Parmesan cheese

1 teaspoon onion powder

1 teaspoon oregano

1 teaspoon basil

1/2 teaspoon salt

28-ounce can tomato sauce

6 cooked lasagna noodles

8 ounces grated soy cheese or low-fat mozzarella cheese (2 1/4 cups grated)

1 tablespoon chopped fresh parsley

Preheat oven to 350°. Combine tofu with spinach, two-thirds of the soy or Parmesan cheese, and onion powder, oregano, basil, and salt. Spread 1/4 cup of tomato sauce in 9 x 13-inch baking dish. Cover with 3 noodles followed by one-half tofu mixture, half of grated cheese, and 1 1/2 cups tomato sauce. Repeat layers with 3 noodles, remaining tofu, tomato sauce, and soy cheese. Sprinkle top with remaining Parmesan. Bake uncovered for 30 to 40 minutes or until the moisture bubbles on the sides of the pan.

Makes 8 servings

FOR 1 SERVING: calories 248, protein: 15 g, carbohydrate: 33 g, fat: 8 g, dietary fiber: 5 g, sodium: 608 mg*

EXCELLENT SOURCE OF: calcium**, iron, vitamin A
GOOD SOURCE OF: magnesium, potassium, folate, niacin, riboflavin, thiamin, vitamins B6 and C

% CALORIES FROM: protein 22%, fat 28%, carbohydrate 49%

* Analysis used Muir Glen organic tomato sauce. Some tomato sauces are much higher in sodium. Salt-free sauces are also available.

** Analysis used tofu set with calcium.

Lemon Ginger Tempeh

Tempeh is a traditional Indonesian soyfood with excellent digestibility and protein quality. Like cheese or wines, tempeh is a fermented product and is generally sold frozen to prevent further fermentation. The seasonings most commonly used with tempeh are garlic and ginger, nicely combined here with lemon. Tempeh can also be marinated using Tofu Marinade (page 110) and used in kebabs or broiled on its own.

3 tablespoons fresh lemon juice

4 teaspoons tamari or soy sauce

2 teaspoons minced ginger

1 teaspoon chopped garlic

1/2 teaspoon onion powder

8 ounces tempeh, sliced in half
   horizontally

1 teaspoon canola oil (if frying)

On a plate, combine lemon juice, tamari, ginger, garlic, and onion powder. Place tempeh slices on plate. Marinate tempeh in the lemon juice mixture in refrigerator for a minimum of 2 hours, turning occasionally and spooning marinade on top. Place tempeh under broiler for 4 minutes, turning after 2 minutes, or fry in oil for about 3 minutes on each side or until brown.

Makes 2 to 3 servings

PER 1/2 RECIPE: calories 264, protein: 23 g, carbohydrate: 23 g, fat: 11 g, dietary fiber: 6 g, sodium: 678 mg

EXCELLENT SOURCE OF: magnesium, niacin, vitamin B$_6$, omega-3 fatty acids
GOOD SOURCE OF: calcium, iron, potassium, zinc, folate, thiamin, vitamin C

% CALORIES FROM: protein 32%, fat 35%, carbohydrate 33%

Lentil Dahl-icious

 Dahl *is an East Indian word for beans, peas, and lentils and the dishes made from using them. In this recipe, the popped mustard seeds and the other Indian spices release their fragrant oils and acids into the dahl when sautéed in oil to create a rich and appetizing dish. Although the dahl is ready to eat when the lentils are soft, best flavor is achieved by simmering on very low heat for 2 hours.*

4 teaspoons canola oil

1 teaspoon mustard seeds

1/2 onion, diced

1 clove garlic, minced

1 teaspoon peeled, minced ginger

1/2 cup tomato paste

1 teaspoon curry powder

1 teaspoon garam masala

1 teaspoon ground cumin

1 teaspoon ground coriander

1 cup dried lentils

2 cups vegetable stock or water

1 cup diced carrots

1 cup diced celery

1/2 teaspoon salt

Heat oil over medium heat in large covered pot; add mustard seeds. Cover and cook for 1 1/2 minutes or until seeds have popped. Add onion, garlic, and ginger; sauté until the onion is soft. Stir in tomato paste, curry powder, garam masala, cumin, and coriander; sauté for 2 to 3 minutes, stirring frequently. Add lentils and stock; cover. Bring to boil, then reduce heat and simmer, covered, for 45 minutes. Add carrots and celery; cook another 20 minutes. Add salt and adjust seasoning.

Makes 4 servings

PER SERVING: calories 274, protein: 16 g, carbohydrate: 43 g, fat: 6 g, dietary fiber: 9 g, sodium: 620 mg

EXCELLENT SOURCE OF: iron, magnesium, potassium, folate, thiamin, vitamin A, B₆, and C

GOOD SOURCE OF: zinc, niacin, riboflavin, vitamin E

% CALORIES FROM: protein 22%, fat 19%, carbohydrate 59%

Mushroom-Lentil Patties

 Supermarkets are stocking a great array of veggie burgers. Check the refrigerator and freezer sections. This homemade rendition, made with lentils and rice, is fresh and full of flavor. Be creative and vary the seasoning, for example with celery seed, cumin, or Cajun spice; serve with Light Mushroom Gravy (page 88) or your favorite tomato sauce.

2 cups water

1/2 cup short-grain brown rice

1/2 cup dried green lentils

2 tablespoons vegetable stock
  or 1 tablespoon canola oil

1/2 onion, diced

12 white mushrooms, sliced

1/4 cup bread crumbs

3 tablespoons chopped fresh
  parsley

2 tablespoons nutritional yeast
  (page 218)

1/2 teaspoon salt

1/4 teaspoon thyme

1/4 teaspoon basil

1/4 teaspoon paprika

Pinch black pepper

1 tablespoon olive oil

In a 1-quart pot, bring water to boil. Add rice and lentils; reduce heat and cook for 50 minutes. Remove from heat, transfer to bowl, and mash with spoon until rice and lentils bind together. Sauté onion and mushrooms in 2 tablespoons stock, adding more stock if necessary, or in 1 tablespoon oil in large pot over medium heat for 5 minutes. Transfer to rice bowl. Stir in bread crumbs, parsley, yeast, salt, thyme, basil, paprika, and pepper, mixing well. Form five 4-inch patties. (An easy way to do this is to line 4-inch wide jar lid with clear wrap, fill lid with patty mix, and turn out onto plate.) Heat oil in skillet over medium heat. Cook patties for 2 to 3 minutes or until golden brown or crispy; flip and cook for 2 to 3 minutes.

Makes 5 patties

PER PATTY: calories 248, protein: 12 g, carbohydrate: 41 g, fat: 5 g, dietary fiber: 5 g, sodium: 332 mg

EXCELLENT SOURCE OF: magnesium, niacin, riboflavin, thiamin, vitamin B_{12}
Good source of: iron, folate

% CALORIES FROM: protein 18%, fat 16%, carbohydrate 66%

Analyzed using Red Star Vegetarian Support Formula Nutritional Yeast

Mushroom Risotto

 This version of a classic Italian dish was developed by chef Michael Fisher. A dear friend and respected colleague, he is talented at developing flavor in vegetarian cuisine. He has created a risotto that is rich and creamy without the traditional use of butter, and enhanced it with the addition of nutritional yeast (page 218). This recipe can serve as the main part of a meal or as a side dish. A serving provides one-quarter of the recommended daily protein intake, based on a body weight of 132 pounds.

5 cups water

2 cups short-grain brown rice

2 cups sliced mushrooms

1/2 cup red pepper, diced

1 onion, diced

2 cloves garlic, minced

1/2 teaspoon salt

1/2 teaspoon dried thyme

1/2 teaspoon dried rosemary

1/8 teaspoon black pepper

1/4 cup nutritional yeast (page 218)

2 tablespoons chopped fresh parsley

2 teaspoons tamari or soy sauce (optional)

Bring water to boil in large covered pot over high heat. Add rice, mushrooms, red pepper, onion, garlic, salt, thyme, rosemary, and pepper. Stir well. Cover and cook for 1 hour over low heat or until water is absorbed by rice. Remove from heat; stir in yeast, parsley, and tamari (if using). Adjust seasoning.

Makes 4 servings

PER SERVING: calories 391, protein: 12 g, carbohydrate: 80 g, fat: 3 g, dietary fiber: 5 g, sodium: 312 mg

EXCELLENT SOURCE OF: magnesium, zinc, folate, niacin, riboflavin, thiamin, vitamins B6, B12*, and C

GOOD SOURCE OF: iron, potassium

% CALORIES FROM: protein 12%, fat 7%, carbohydrate 81%

*Analyzed using Red Star Vegetarian Support Formula Nutritional Yeast

Open-Face Tofu Sandwich

 Sandwiches are a popular way to take in daily nourishment and are often eaten on the run. Since they are so common they can become mundane. Not this one! Eaten with a knife and fork, this sandwich is taken out of the domain of the ordinary and into the realm of the elegant.

4–6 slices firm tofu, 1/4-inch thick	2 slices whole-wheat bread
2 teaspoons light or regular soy sauce or tamari	8 slices cucumber
	4 slices tomato
2 tablespoons mayonnaise (Tofu, page 111, or commercial)	Pinch pepper
	1/2 cup alfalfa sprouts (optional)

Marinate sliced tofu in soy sauce or tamari on plate for 5 minutes. Warm tofu on medium heat for 1 minute in skillet, turning once. Spread mayonnaise on bread slices. Arrange tofu on bread followed by cucumber and tomato slices. Sprinkle with pepper to taste. Garnish with sprouts (if using).

Makes 2 sandwiches

PER SANDWICH: calories 358, protein: 27g, carbohydrate: 38 g, fat, 13 g dietary fiber: 8 g, sodium: 720 mg

EXCELLENT SOURCE OF: calcium, iron, magnesium, potassium, zinc, folate, riboflavin, thiamin, vitamin C
GOOD SOURCE OF: niacin, vitamin B_6

% CALORIES FROM: protein 28%, fat 31%, carbohydrate 41%

Savory Black Bean Stew

 This delicious recipe is a splendid example of the balance between protein, fat, and carbohydrate recommended in the dietary guidelines (see the first chapter). Served with Quinoa Salad (page 98) or with fresh rolls and a little Morocc-Un-Butter (page 79), this iron-rich stew is a very fortifying lunch or supper. It also makes a great combination with rice, rolled up in a soft Mexican tortilla with salsa and fresh cilantro.

1 cup vegetable stock	1 teaspoon dried basil
1 tablespoon canola oil (optional)	1 teaspoon chili powder
1 cup diced celery	1 teaspoon ground cumin
1 cup diced carrots	1 teaspoon ground coriander
1/2 onion, diced	1/2 teaspoon salt
1 clove garlic, minced	1/4 teaspoon pepper
3 cups cooked black beans	1/4 cup chopped fresh cilantro
1 cup fresh or canned tomatoes	1 tablespoon lime juice
1/4 cup tomato paste	

Sauté celery, carrots, onion, and garlic in 2 tablespoons of the stock, adding more stock if necessary, or in 1 tablespoon oil in large pot over medium heat for 5 minutes. Stir in remaining stock, beans, tomatoes, paste, basil, chili, cumin, coriander, salt, and pepper; cover and simmer for 20 minutes. Simmer, uncovered, for 20 minutes, adding more stock if needed to just cover beans. Just before serving, stir in fresh cilantro and lime juice. Season to taste.

Makes 5 servings

PER SERVING: calories 199, protein: 11 g, carbohydrate: 39 g, fat: 1 g, dietary fiber: 9 g, sodium: 401 mg
WITH OIL: calories 223, fat 4 g

EXCELLENT SOURCE OF: iron, magnesium, potassium, folate, thiamin, vitamins A and C
GOOD SOURCE OF: calcium, vitamin B6

% CALORIES FROM: protein 21%, fat 4%, carbohydrate 75%
WITH OIL: % CALORIES FROM: protein 19%, fat 14%, carbohydrate 67%

Stuffed Winter Squash

 In some families or groups of friends, getting together to cook is one of the best parts of a celebration. Assembling this stuffing and baked squash can be the central activity for a wonderful day spent with the people you love. Serve it with Light Mushroom Gravy (page 188) or Rosemary Gravy (page 189) plus other items from the Thanksgiving and Christmas Menu Selections (page 54). Choose a squash such as hubbard, butternut, or acorn. Two or three smaller squashes work too if you can't find a single large one, as referred to in this recipe.

This stuffing can be used to stuff any vegetable. You may want to experiment with different grains such as quinoa, buckwheat, or couscous to replace the rice; legumes such as lentils to replace the millet; and cashews or almonds instead of sunflower seeds.

1 winter squash (5 pounds)

Stuffing

1 1/2 cups cooked brown rice

1 1/2 cups cooked millet

2 tablespoons stock or
   1 tablespoon canola oil

2 stalks celery, diced

1/2 onion, diced

2 cloves garlic, minced

1 cup corn kernels, fresh, canned,
   or frozen

1/2 cup diced sweet red pepper

1/2 cup sunflower seeds
   (optional)

1/4 cup chopped fresh parsley

1 teaspoon dried oregano

1 teaspoon dried thyme

1/2 teaspoon sage

1/2 teaspoon celery seed

2–3 tablespoons tamari or
   soy sauce

1/4–1/2 teaspoon salt

1/8 teaspoon pepper

Preheat oven to 350°. Pierce top of squash with sharp knife at 45 degree angle. Pushing knife blade away from your body, rotate blade around top of squash and remove cone-shaped top piece. Remove any fibrous material from cone and set top aside. Remove seeds and pulp from cavity of squash with soup spoon. Set squash and top on baking pan and bake for 30 minutes. Remove squash and lid from oven and set aside to cool for 15 minutes.

Assembly

Combine rice and millet in large bowl and set aside to cool. Sauté celery, onion, and garlic in 2 tablespoons of stock, adding more stock if necessary, or in 1 tablespoon oil in large pot over medium heat for 5 minutes or until onions are soft. Transfer to grains bowl, along with corn, red pepper, sunflower seeds (if using), parsley, oregano, thyme, sage, celery seeds, tamari, salt, and pepper. Stir together and adjust seasoning.

Spoon stuffing into cavity of squash until almost full. Set lid in place, and return squash to baking pan and bake for 45 to 60 minutes or until toothpick can be inserted easily into squash. If you have leftover stuffing, place in loaf pan, sprinkle with 2 to 3 tablespoons of stock or water, cover, and heat through for last 20 minutes of squash cooking time. Remove squash from oven and place on warm serving platter. Slice into wedges.

Makes 5 cups stuffing, 5 hearty servings

PER SERVING: calories 355, protein: 10 g, carbohydrate: 76 g, fat: 4 g, dietary fiber: 16 g, sodium: 545 mg

EXCELLENT SOURCE OF: magnesium, potassium, folate, thiamin, niacin, vitamins A, B_6, and C
GOOD SOURCE OF: iron, zinc, riboflavin

% CALORIES FROM: protein 10%, fat 10%, carbohydrate 80%

Sushi

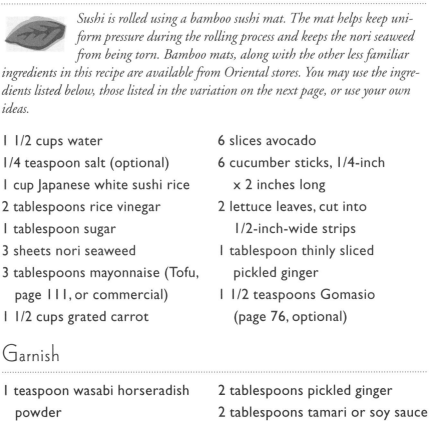

Sushi is rolled using a bamboo sushi mat. The mat helps keep uniform pressure during the rolling process and keeps the nori seaweed from being torn. Bamboo mats, along with the other less familiar ingredients in this recipe are available from Oriental stores. You may use the ingredients listed below, those listed in the variation on the next page, or use your own ideas.

1 1/2 cups water	6 slices avocado
1/4 teaspoon salt (optional)	6 cucumber sticks, 1/4-inch
1 cup Japanese white sushi rice	x 2 inches long
2 tablespoons rice vinegar	2 lettuce leaves, cut into
1 tablespoon sugar	1/2-inch-wide strips
3 sheets nori seaweed	1 tablespoon thinly sliced
3 tablespoons mayonnaise (Tofu,	pickled ginger
page 111, or commercial)	1 1/2 teaspoons Gomasio
1 1/2 cups grated carrot	(page 76, optional)

Garnish

1 teaspoon wasabi horseradish	2 tablespoons pickled ginger
powder	2 tablespoons tamari or soy sauce
Water	

Bring water with salt (if using) to boil. Rinse rice and add to water. Cover, reduce heat, and simmer for 20 minutes. In small bowl combine rice vinegar and sugar. Drizzle vinegar mixture over cooked rice, mixing with fork. Set aside to cool completely before assembling rolls. Set out all ingredients needed for rolls on counter. Lay down sheet of nori on bamboo sushi mat.

Spoon 3/4 cup of rice over sushi sheet as shown in the Making Sushi photo sequence (see color photos), leaving 1-inch border at bottom and top and spooning rice out to right and left edges. Spread one-third of the mayonnaise over the rice in a single strip near bottom of nori. Layer one-third of carrots, avocado, cucumber, lettuce, ginger, and Gomasio (if using) over mayonnaise. Dip index finger into bowl of water and moisten top edge of nori sheet to ensure seal. Using both hands and firm pressure, lift mat and roll like jelly roll until sushi roll is formed. Repeat until all three rolls have been assembled.

Place roll on cutting board, seam side down; trim ends of any food that squeezed out during rolling process. Cut roll into 8 equal pieces using a serrated knife; arrange on platter.

In small bowl, mix wasabi powder with a few drops of water, gradually adding more water until smooth paste forms. Place wasabi paste on platter along with pickled ginger. Serve with small bowl of tamari.

VARIATION: Brown rice may be used in place of white rice. Use 1 cup of brown rice to 2 cups of water and cook for 45 minutes. Replace sugar with same amount of Sucanat (page 219) or brown sugar.

Makes 3 rolls; 8 pieces per roll.

PER ROLL (1/3 RECIPE), WITHOUT GARNISHES: calories 305, protein: 6 g, carbohydrate: 61 g, fat: 4 g, dietary fiber: 5 g, sodium: 66 mg

EXCELLENT SOURCE OF: vitamin A
GOOD SOURCE OF: iron, magnesium, potassium, niacin, thiamin, vitamins B$_6$ and C

% CALORIES FROM: protein 8%, fat 12%, carbohydrate 80%

Sweet and Sour Tofu

 Rice vinegar can be smoother, milder, and sweeter than vinegar made from fruit. It works well in this stir-fry as the amount of sweetener used for the sweet and sour effect is reduced. The result is that the flavor of the vegetables is not masked by the sauce. Best served on a bed of rice, this recipe on its own will easily feed two hungry adults, or four if the meal includes other items.

2 tablespoons vegetable stock
   or 1 tablespoon canola oil
1 cup diced onion
1 cup diagonally sliced carrots
1 cup diced sweet red pepper
1 cup diced sweet green pepper
2 cloves garlic, minced
1 tablespoon peeled, minced
   gingerroot
1/2 cup diced pineapple

3/4 cup pineapple juice
1/4 cup Sucanat (page 219)
   or brown sugar
3 tablespoons rice vinegar
2 tablespoons tamari or soy
   sauce
1 tablespoon cornstarch
1 cup diced firm tofu
1 tablespoon chopped fresh
   parsley

Sauté onions, carrots, peppers, garlic, and ginger in 2 tablespoons of stock, adding more stock if necessary, or in 1 tablespoon oil in skillet over medium heat for 5 minutes. Add pineapple.

Mix together pineapple juice, sugar, vinegar, tamari, and cornstarch and add to skillet along with tofu, stirring constantly until thickened. Simmer, covered, for 3 minutes. Garnish with parsley.

Makes 4 servings

PER SERVING: calories 201, protein: 12 g, carbohydrate: 29 g,
fat: 6 g, dietary fiber: 5 g, sodium: 44 mg
WITH OIL: calories 231, fat 9 g

EXCELLENT SOURCE OF: calcium*, iron, vitamins A, B6, and C, omega-3 fatty acids
GOOD SOURCE OF: magnesium, potassium, folate, thiamin

% CALORIES FROM: protein 22%, fat 25%, carbohydrate 53%
WITH OIL: % CALORIES FROM: protein 19%, fat 34%, carbohydrate 47%

*Analyzed using tofu set with calcium.

Szechuan Vegetables over Buckwheat Noodles

Szechuan province in western China is famous for the spicy hot food that has been developed using combinations of chili and other spices. This dish is spiced mildly; you can make it hotter by increasing the amounts of chili and ginger. Buckwheat is in fact not a wheat, but is the seed of a plant in the rhubarb family.

8 ounces buckwheat noodles

1 tablespoon canola oil

1 cup sliced mushrooms

1 onion, chopped in 1/2-inch pieces

2 cloves garlic, minced

1–2 teaspoons peeled, minced gingerroot

1 cup sliced carrots

1 cup broccoli florets

1 cup water

1/4 cup black bean sauce

1 tablespoon cornstarch

1/4–1/2 teaspoon fresh chopped chili peppers or chili sauce

2 teaspoons tamari or soy sauce (optional)

2 cups bean sprouts

1 cup snow peas

2 tablespoons chopped fresh cilantro

Cook noodles in boiling water for 5 to 8 minutes or until tender. Drain. Meanwhile, in wok, sauté mushrooms, onion, garlic, and ginger in oil over medium heat for 5 minutes. Stir in carrots and broccoli; cook for 3 to 5 minutes or until vegetables are tender-crisp. In small bowl combine water, black bean sauce, cornstarch, chili, and tamari (if using). Reduce heat to low; stir cornstarch mixture into wok along with bean sprouts and snow peas. Cover and cook for 2 to 3 minutes once liquid has come to a boil, stirring once or twice. Garnish with cilantro.

Makes 3 servings

PER SERVING: calories 425, protein: 18 g, carbohydrate: 81 g, fat: 7 g, dietary fiber: 7 g, sodium: 881 mg

EXCELLENT SOURCE OF: iron, magnesium, potassium, folate, niacin, riboflavin, thiamin, vitamins A and C
GOOD SOURCE OF: calcium, zinc

% CALORIES FROM: protein 16%, fat 13%, carbohydrate 71%

Ten Tasty Ways to Stuff Your Pita Pockets

- Avocado Dip (page 72), tomato and sprouts
- Black Bean Hummus (page 73) with salsa and quinoa or rice
- Gee Whiz Spread (page 75), diced cucumbers, and finely shredded lettuce
- Hummus (page 78), tomato, lettuce, and Cucumber Dill Dressing (page 104)
- Couscous Salad (page 92), Lemon-Tahini Dressing (page 106), and chopped lettuce
- Mashed chick-peas (or falafels from mix), Lemon-Tahini Dressing (page 106), sprouts, and diced tomatoes
- Mexican Rice (page 176), lettuce, salsa, and soy or Cheddar cheese
- Quinoa Salad (page 98), lettuce, and chick-peas
- Pesto-the-Best-Oh! (page 80) and sprouts
- Basmati Rice Salad (page 89), Tamarind Date Sauce (page 191), diced tomatoes, and chopped lettuce

The following are particularly low in fat:

- Black Bean Hummus (page 73) with salsa and quinoa or rice
- Low-Fat Variation of Hummus (page 78), tomato, and lettuce
- Low-Fat Variation of Hummus (page 78), Couscous Salad (page 92, without tahini)
- Roasted Garlic and Yam Spread (page 82) with diced sweet red, yellow, or green pepper
- Mexican Rice (page 176), lettuce, and salsa
- Quinoa Salad without oil (page 98), lettuce, and chick-peas

Teriyaki Tofu

 Teriyaki Sauce (page 192) strikes a balance between saltiness and sweetness. Native to Japan, teriyaki sauce is a once-in-a-while sauce as it can be high in sodium. Served over a bed of whole-grain rice or your favorite noodles, this recipe makes a fully satisfying, attractive meal.

2 tablespoons vegetable stock
　or 1 tablespoon canola oil

1 cup diced carrots

1 cup diced daikon radish

1/2 onion, diced

1 clove garlic, minced

1 teaspoon minced peeled
　gingerroot

1 cup sweet red peppers

1 cup sweet green peppers

1 cup diced firm tofu

1 cup Teriyaki Sauce (page 192)

1–2 tablespoons chopped fresh
　cilantro

In large skillet sauté carrots, radish, onion, garlic, and ginger in 2 tablespoons of stock, adding more stock if necessary, or in 1 tablespoon oil over medium heat for 5 minutes. Stir in peppers and tofu; sauté for 3 minutes. Pour in teriyaki sauce; cover and simmer for 2 to 3 minutes. Garnish with cilantro.

Makes 4 servings

PER SERVING: calories 218, protein: 13 g, carbohydrate: 27 g, fat: 6 g, alcohol 3 g, dietary fiber: 5 g, sodium: 553 mg
WITH OIL: calories: 248, fat 9 g

EXCELLENT SOURCE OF: calcium, iron, vitamins A, B₆, and C
GOOD SOURCE OF: magnesium, potassium, folate, thiamin, omega-3 fatty acids

% CALORIES FROM: protein 22%, fat 22%, carbohydrate 48%, alcohol 8%
WITH OIL: % CALORIES FROM: protein 20%, fat 31%, carbohydrate 42%, alcohol 7%

*Analyzed using tofu set with calcium, and with sake as an ingredient in the Teriyaki Sauce.

Tofu—An Easy Entrée

 Tofu is Asia's number one fast food. For a good source of dietary calcium, select a tofu package with calcium on its ingredient list.
Drawing on the endless variety of Oriental sauces well suited to tofu, we have provided recipes for low-fat Teriyaki Sauce (page 192) and the heartier Spicy Peanut Sauce (page 190). The next time you go shopping, look for Thai, vegetarian oyster, garlic-chili and other exotic sauces. Look for Annie's, a Vermont company that makes a line of delicious and outstanding low-fat sauces.

12-ounce block extra firm tofu

1/3 to 1/2 cup your favorite sauce

Preheat oven to 350°. Drain tofu and cut into 1/4-inch-thick slices. Place tofu slices, touching each other, on lightly oiled or nonstick pan. Spread with sauce. Bake for 20 minutes or until the sauce begins to glaze.

VARIATION: Cut tofu into 1-inch cubes. Place in pan with sauce and heat through.

Vegetable Kabobs

The assorted vegetables listed in this recipe, assembled on a skewer, make a colorful addition to a picnic or beach barbecue. The use of Tofu Marinade provides a burst a flavor. Serve in a pita pocket with Cucumber Dressing (page 104) or on a bed of rice.

16-ounce package extra-firm tofu	1 zucchini
Tofu Marinade (page 110)	16 small mushrooms
1 sweet red pepper	8 cherry tomatoes

Cut tofu into 3/4-inch cubes. Cover with marinade and refrigerate for 4 to 6 hours.

Cut pepper and zucchini into same size pieces as tofu. (You should have 16 pieces each of peppers and zucchini.) Starting and ending with mushrooms, thread vegetables onto eight 10-inch bamboo skewers. (NOTE: The skewer will burn if a space is left between vegetables, so thread food snugly.) One possible sequence would be: mushroom, red pepper, tofu, zucchini, tofu, cherry tomato, tofu, zucchini, tofu, red pepper, mushroom. Grill skewers or place on baking sheet 6 inches under the broiler for 10 minutes, turning and basting occasionally with marinade.

Makes 4 servings, 2 kabobs per serving

Veggie Pepperoni Pizza

 Pizza can be a wonderful balance of nutritious foods; look at all the vitamins and minerals in this one! It can be served as a quick and easy lunch, supper, or snack for children of all ages. For adults, be creative and use more exotic ingredients like artichokes, soaked sun-dried tomatoes, or capers.

4 pita bread (each 6-inch)
   or pizza shells

1 cup tomato sauce

8 slices (5 ounces) Yves veggie
   pepperoni, quartered

12 thin slices tomato

1/2 red onion, sliced thinly

1/2 green pepper, sliced thinly

4–6 mushrooms, sliced

8 black olives, sliced

1/4 cup sliced green onions

1/4 cup grated soy cheese or
   Parmesan cheese

4 teaspoons chopped fresh basil

Preheat oven to 375°. Place pita bread on a lightly oiled pan or silicon paper. Cover pita bread with tomato sauce. Evenly distribute pepperoni followed by tomato slices, onion, green pepper, and mushrooms. Garnish with olives and green onions, then sprinkle with cheese. Bake for 10 to 12 minutes or until browned. Top with fresh basil, and cut each pizza into quarters.

Makes 4 pizzas

PER PIZZA: calories 294, protein: 9 g, carbohydrate: 51 g, fat: 4 g, dietary fiber: 9 g, sodium: 803 mg

EXCELLENT SOURCE OF: iron, thiamin, vitamin C
GOOD SOURCE OF: magnesium, potassium, folate, niacin, riboflavin, vitamins A and B6

% CALORIES FROM: protein 13%, fat 12%, carbohydrate 75%

Zucchini Stuffed with Lentils and Bulgur

 Zucchini is one of the most abundant of the summer squashes and it can be easily grown in the garden or on a sunny balcony. This lentil, bulgur, and dill stuffing may also be used to fill other vegetables such as sweet peppers, eggplant, squash, or tomatoes.

1/2 cup dry lentils

1 1/2 cups water

1/2 small onion, diced

1 clove garlic, minced

1/4 cup bulgur

1/2 cup tomato juice

2 zucchini, each approximately
   8" x 2–1/2"

2 tablespoons chopped parsley

2 tablespoons lemon juice

3/4 teaspoon dillweed

1/4 teaspoon salt

Pinch black pepper

Bring lentils, water, onion, and garlic to a boil in covered pot; reduce heat and simmer for 45 minutes. Heat tomato juice; pour over bulgur in bowl and let soak for 15 minutes.

Preheat oven to 350°. Halve zucchinis lengthwise and, using teaspoon, scoop out and discard pulp starting 1 inch from either end, leaving shell 1/2-inch thick.

To make stuffing, combine lentil mixture, soaked bulgur, parsley, lemon juice, dillweed, salt, and pepper. Mix well and adjust seasoning. Place stuffing in cavity of zucchinis, set on baking sheet and bake for 20 to 30 minutes or until zucchini is soft.

Makes 4 servings

PER SERVING: calories 167, protein: 10 g, carbohydrate: 34 g, fat: 0.6 g, dietary fiber: 13 g, sodium: 272 mg

EXCELLENT SOURCE OF: iron, magnesium, potassium, folate, vitamins B6 and C
GOOD SOURCE OF: zinc, niacin, riboflavin, thiamin

% Calories from: protein 22%, fat 3%, carbohydrate 75%

Side Dishes

Baked Potato and Fixings

What can you do with a baked potato if you don't load it up with butter and sour cream? Here are a wealth of new ideas to brighten up your dinner table. In fact, with a variety of these toppings, you can build a meal around baked potatoes by adding soup or salad. Potatoes bake very well without oil; however, coating with a minimal amount will soften the skin, which some people prefer.

1 russet or similar baking potato, washed

1/4 teaspoon canola oil (optional)

Rub oil (if using) over potato.

OVEN METHOD: Pierce potato 3 to 4 times with fork, place in 375° oven, and bake for about 45 minutes or until soft when skewer is inserted into potato.

MICROWAVE METHOD: Heat 1 potato on high for about 5 minutes, depending on size of potato.

Low-Calorie Toppings

Cut an x on top of potato and top with any of the following suggestions.
- Cucumber Dill Dressing (page 104)
- Salsa
- Salt and freshly cracked pepper
- Diced red peppers, tomato, and cucumber
- Dulse or kelp powder/flakes
- Fresh chopped herbs (parsley, basil, etc.)
- Gomasio (page 76)
- Light Mushroom Gravy (page 188)
- Veggie (soy-based) bacon bits
- Your favorite low-fat salad dressing
- Nutritional yeast (page 218)

Creamy Smooth Toppings

- Avocado Dip (page 72)
- Caesar Dressing (page 90)
- Extra virgin olive oil
- Flaxseed oil
- Grated soy cheese
- Lemon Tahini Dressing (page 106)
- Miso, thinned with a little water
- Morocc-Un-Butter (page 79)
- Pesto-the-Best-Oh! (page 80)
- Raspberry Vinaigrette (page 109)
- Rosemary Gravy (page 189)

Baked Eggplant

 This recipe is similar to Crispy Tofu Fingers (page 132) in that it incorporates seasoned nutritional yeast as the coating for the eggplant. Since eggplant is porous it absorbs liquid or oil quite readily. Dredge the sliced eggplant very briefly (do not let it sit in the soy sauce otherwise the eggplant will absorb too much salt). Any combination of Middle Eastern spices with the yeast works well with eggplant: cumin, paprika, coriander, cayenne, turmeric, and garlic powder. Serve this vegetable on its own or with a tomato sauce. Any leftover yeast mixture can be used in soups and casseroles or sprinkled over fresh, hot popcorn.

1 eggplant, cut in 1/2" slices	1 teaspoon ground cumin
1–2 tablespoons light soy sauce or regular tamari	1 teaspoon garlic powder
	1 teaspoon paprika
1/4 cup nutritional yeast (page 218)	1 teaspoon vegetable oil for baking sheet

Preheat oven to 350°. Arrange on counter, sliced eggplant, flat-bottomed soup bowl containing soy sauce or tamari, another bowl containing yeast mixed with seasonings, and a nonstick or lightly oiled baking sheet. Dip eggplant slices into tamari and then into seasoned yeast to coat both sides. Place slices on baking sheet and bake for 15 to 20 minutes.

Makes 4–6 servings

PER SERVING: calories 63, protein: 5 g, carbohydrate: 12 g, fat: 0.8 g, dietary fiber: 4 g, sodium: 233 mg

EXCELLENT SOURCE OF: folate, niacin, riboflavin, thiamin, vitamins B$_6$ and B$_{12}$*
GOOD SOURCE OF: potassium

% CALORIES FROM: protein 25%, fat 10%, carbohydrate 65%

*Analyzed using Red Star Vegetarian Support Formula Nutritional Yeast

Bok Choy, Mushrooms, and Ginger

 Oriental greens such as bok choy are becoming popular with Westerners as a result of scientific evidence of their content of highly absorbable calcium. As you'll see from the nutritional analysis, there are plenty of vitamins as well.

2 teaspoons toasted sesame oil

2 cups sliced mushrooms

1 clove garlic, minced

2 teaspoons peeled, minced gingerroot

6 cups sliced bok choy

1 tablespoon tamari or soy sauce

In wok or large skillet, sauté mushrooms in sesame oil over medium-high heat for 4 to 5 minutes. Add garlic, ginger, and bok choy; sauté for 5 minutes or until the stems of bok choy are tender-crisp. Stir in tamari and serve.

Makes 4 servings

PER SERVING: calories 53, protein: 3 g, carbohydrate: 5 g, fat: 3 g, dietary fiber: 2 g, sodium: 238 mg

EXCELLENT SOURCE OF: folate, vitamins A and C
GOOD SOURCE OF: calcium, potassium, niacin, riboflavin, and vitamin B6

% CALORIES FROM: protein 20%, fat 46%, carbohydrate 34%

Carrots and Broccoli with Hijiki

 Hijiki, also known as hiziki, is a black seaweed rich in trace minerals. In this stir-fry it contrasts visually with the bright green broccoli and the deep orange carrots. Toasted sesame oil brings a rich, nutty flavor that blends exceptionally well with hijiki. Rice syrup is a mild, subtle sweetener that takes the edge off the strong-tasting hijiki.

1/4 cup dried hijiki seaweed

2 tablespoons vegetable stock
   or 1 tablespoon canola oil

1 red onion, chopped

1 clove garlic, minced

1 teaspoon minced, peeled
   gingerroot

1 1/2 cups sliced carrots

1 1/2 cups broccoli florets

1/4 teaspoon toasted sesame oil

1 teaspoon tamari or soy sauce

1 tablespoon rice syrup or honey

Cover hijiki in bowl with 1 cup of water for at least 15 minutes. Rinse under cold water. In large skillet, sauté onion, garlic, and ginger in 2 tablespoons stock, adding more stock if necessary, or in 1 tablespoon oil over medium heat for 5 minutes or until onions are soft. Add carrots, broccoli, and sesame oil; sauté for 5 to 8 minutes or until vegetables are tender-crisp. Stir in rinsed hijiki, tamari, and sweetener.

Makes 4 servings

PER SERVING: calories: 86, protein: 3 g, carbohydrate: 19 g, fat: 0.8 g, dietary fiber: 5 g, sodium: 195 mg
WITH OIL: calories: 116, fat: 4 g

EXCELLENT SOURCE OF: vitamins A and C
GOOD SOURCE OF: calcium, potassium, folate, vitamin B$_6$

% CALORIES FROM: protein 15%, fat 7%, carbohydrate 78%
WITH OIL: % CALORIES FROM: protein 11%, fat 30%, carbohydrate 59%

Cauliflower and Yam

 Powdered spices such as curry powder and mustard seeds are heated in a small amount of oil to release their volatile oils, making the dish fragrant and flavorful.

4 teaspoons canola oil

1 teaspoon mustard seeds

1/2 onion, sliced

1 teaspoon curry powder

1 teaspoon coriander seeds, crushed, or 1/2 teaspoon ground coriander

2 cups cauliflower florets cut into bite-size pieces

2 cups diced yams

3/4 cup water

1/4 teaspoon salt

Heat mustard seeds in oil over medium heat in covered pot or skillet. As soon as seeds have popped (1–2 minutes), stir in onion, curry powder, and coriander seeds; sauté for 3 to 4 minutes. Stir in cauliflower, yams, water, and salt, stirring well. Cover and simmer for 15 minutes or until vegetables are tender-crisp.

Makes 4 servings

PER SERVING: calories 155, protein: 3 g, carbohydrate: 26 g, fat: 5 g, dietary fiber: 4 g, sodium: 162 mg

EXCELLENT SOURCE OF: potassium, vitamins A and C
GOOD SOURCE OF: folate, vitamin B$_6$

% CALORIES FROM: protein 7%, fat 29%, carbohydrate 64%

Corn with Red Peppers

 What a pleasure it is when the season for fresh corn arrives! This gold and red vegetable combination goes well with Savory Black Bean Stew (page 147) and either Quinoa Salad (page 98) or a steaming plate of rice. To remove corn from the ear, slice off the stem and place the ear of corn, stem end down, on a damp cloth to avoid slipping. Remove kernels by slicing from top to bottom all around the ear. One large ear will produce about 1 cup of corn.

2 tablespoons vegetable stock
    or 1 tablespoon canola oil

1/2 red onion, chopped

1 clove garlic, minced

3 cups fresh, canned, or
    frozen corn kernels

1/3 cup diced sweet red pepper

1/8 teaspoon salt

Pinch pepper

Sauté onion and garlic in 2 tablespoons of stock, adding more stock if necessary, or in 1 tablespoon oil over medium heat for 3 to 5 minutes or until onions are soft. Add corn, sweet pepper, salt, and pepper. Cover and cook for 5 minutes. Adjust seasoning.

Makes 4 servings

PER SERVING: calories 114, protein: 4 g, carbohydrate: 28 g, fat: 0.6 g, dietary fiber: 4 g, sodium: 80 mg
WITH OIL: calories 144, fat 4 g

EXCELLENT SOURCE OF: vitamin C
GOOD SOURCE OF: folate, vitamins A and B$_6$

% CALORIES FROM: protein 13%, fat 1%, carbohydrate 86%
WITH OIL: % CALORIES FROM: protein 10%, fat 22%, carbohydrate 68%

Currant and Cumin Pilaf

Small sweet grapes, dried to form currants, are often an ingredient in Middle Eastern pilafs. Cumin combines here with currants and cloves to create a satisfying dish to serve with Vegetable Kabobs (page 157).

4 cups water

2 cups brown rice

2/3 cup currants

1 teaspoon ground cumin

1/2 teaspoon salt

1/4 teaspoon turmeric

6 whole cloves

1/4 cup finely chopped green onion

Boil water in covered pot over high heat; add rice, currants, cumin, salt, turmeric, and cloves; stir well. Cover, reduce heat, and cook for 45 minutes. Just before serving, stir in green onions.

Makes 4 servings

PER SERVING: calories 421, protein: 9 g, carbohydrate: 91 g, fat: 3 g, dietary fiber: 5 g, sodium: 309 g

EXCELLENT SOURCE OF: magnesium, niacin, thiamin, vitamin B6
GOOD SOURCE OF: iron, zinc

% CALORIES FROM: protein 8%, fat 6%, carbohydrate 86%

Dijon Scalloped Potatoes

 Scalloped potatoes are generally made with loads of milk, cream, and butter. This version is dairy-free and the fat content (from oil and miso) has been kept fairly low. Miso combined with Dijon mustard gives the dish a distinctly different appeal. Use unpeeled potatoes to retain the fiber and nutritional value that reside in the skin.

2 tablespoons miso

1 tablespoon Dijon mustard

1/8 teaspoon pepper

4 potatoes (unpeeled)

1/2 red onion

1/4 cup unbleached or
   all-purpose flour

2 tablespoons oil

2 cups vegetable stock

2 tablespoons bread crumbs

In small bowl, combine miso, mustard, and pepper, mixing until miso is dissolved. Cut 2 potatoes into 1/4-inch slices and layer in a lightly oiled 8-inch square baking dish. Thinly slice onion and spread over potatoes. Slice remaining 2 potatoes and spread over onions.

In saucepan over medium heat, combine flour and oil; cook for 3 minutes, stirring frequently to prevent flour from burning. Set aside to cool for 3 minutes. Return to heat and stir continuously while gradually pouring stock into saucepan. Bring to boil, reduce heat, and cook for 10 minutes, stirring occasionally.

Preheat oven to 375°. When sauce is cooked, remove from heat, stir in miso mixture, and adjust seasoning. Pour over potatoes, cover with foil, and bake for 30 minutes. Remove foil, sprinkle potatoes evenly with bread crumbs, and return to oven uncovered for 20 minutes or until potatoes are cooked.

Makes 6 servings

PER SERVING: calories 165, protein: 4 g, carbohydrate: 27 g, fat: 5 g, dietary fiber: 3 g, sodium: 298 mg

GOOD SOURCE OF: potassium, thiamin, vitamin B$_6$

% CALORIES FROM: protein 8%, fat 27%, carbohydrate 65%

Green Beans with Black Beans

 Black bean sauce can be found in small jars at Oriental grocers and in most supermarkets. The sauce is combined here with green beans but try it with other vegetables such as bok choy, napa (Chinese) cabbage, or tomatoes.

2 tablespoons vegetable stock
   or 2 teaspoons canola oil

1/2 onion, chopped

1 clove garlic, minced

2 cups chopped fresh or canned
   tomatoes (drained)

2 cups diagonally sliced green
   beans

2 tablespoons black bean sauce

2 teaspoons slivered almonds
   or sesame seeds (optional)

Sauté onions, garlic, and tomatoes in 2 tablespoons of stock, adding more stock if necessary, or in 2 teaspoons oil in skillet over medium heat for 8 to 10 minutes to soften the onions and tomatoes. Add green beans, and continue cooking for 3 to 4 minutes until green beans are tender-crisp. Stir in black bean sauce; garnish with almonds or sesame seeds (if using).

Makes 4 servings

PER SERVING: calories 60, protein: 3 g, carbohydrate: 13 g, fat: 0.7 g, dietary fiber: 4 g, sodium: 263 mg
WITH OIL AND ALMONDS: calories: 126, Fat 7g

EXCELLENT SOURCE OF: vitamin C
GOOD SOURCE OF: potassium, vitamin A

% CALORIES FROM: protein 16%, fat 10%, carbohydrate 74%
WITH OIL AND ALMONDS: % CALORIES FROM: protein 13%, fat 33%, carbohydrate 54%

Greens with Tomatoes and Garlic

This exceptional, nutritionally well-balanced dish can be a back-bone of your calcium-rich recipes, with approximately 200 milligrams of highly available calcium per serving. The vitamin C in the tomatoes helps our bodies to absorb another mineral in the kale, iron. Furthermore, the combination tastes very good indeed!

8 cups sliced kale greens	1/2 teaspoon dried basil
2 cups chopped fresh or	1/2 teaspoon dried oregano
canned tomatoes (drained)	1/4 teaspoon salt
1 clove garlic, minced	Pinch pepper

Remove stems from kale; chop kale leaves into bite-size pieces. Set aside. In skillet, sauté tomatoes, garlic, basil, and oregano over medium heat until most of the liquid from tomatoes has evaporated, about 3 to 5 minutes. Add kale greens, salt, and pepper to skillet; cover and cook for 2 minutes. Adjust seasoning.

Makes 4 servings

PER SERVING: calories 72, protein: 5 g, carbohydrate: 15 g, fat: 1 g, dietary fiber: 3 g, sodium: 204 mg

EXCELLENT SOURCE OF: vitamins A, C, E
GOOD SOURCE OF: calcium, iron, magnesium, folate, riboflavin, thiamin, vitamin B$_6$

% CALORIES FROM: protein 22%, fat 10%, carbohydrate 68%

Kale and Red Pepper Holly Ring

 The deep green kale tossed with bright red bell peppers resembles a holly wreath when presented in a circle on a plate. This simple yet elegant dish is perfect for the holiday season and adds color and a festive touch any time of the year.

6 cups thinly sliced kale greens

1/4 cup diced sweet red pepper

2 tablespoons flaxseed oil
  (optional)

1 tablespoon balsamic vinegar

1 tablespoon tamari or soy sauce

Place kale in steamer; sprinkle with red pepper. Cover and steam over medium-high heat until the peppers are tender-crisp. Drain. Combine flaxseed oil (if using), vinegar, and tamari in a bowl large enough to hold kale. Toss kale and peppers into vinegar mixture and place on warm platter. Create wreath shape by pushing kale toward edges of platter, leaving an open space in center.

Makes 4 servings

PER SERVING: calories 56, protein: 4 g, carbohydrate: 11 g, fat: 0.7 g, dietary fiber: 2 g, sodium: 295 mg.
WITH FLAXSEED OIL: calories 121, fat 8 g

EXCELLENT SOURCE OF: vitamins A and C
GOOD SOURCE OF: calcium, iron, potassium, vitamin B_6

% CALORIES FROM: protein 23%, fat 10%, carbohydrate 67%
WITH FLAXSEED OIL: % CALORIES FROM: protein 12%, fat 54%, carbohydrate 34%

With flaxseed oil this dish becomes an excellent source of omega-3 fatty acids

Lemon Roasted Potatoes

 The Greeks make spectacular but high-fat roasted potatoes using stock, seasonings, lemon, and olive oil. This version keeps the lemon and herb flavor but greatly reduces the oil and salt.

6 potatoes (unpeeled)

2 tablespoons lemon juice

1 tablespoon extra-virgin olive oil

2 tablespoons chopped fresh parsley

1 teaspoon dried basil

1/2 teaspoon dried oregano

1/2 teaspoon salt

1/4 teaspoon pepper

Preheat oven to 350°. Wash potatoes and cut each potato into 8 uniform pieces. Combine lemon juice, olive oil, parsley, basil, oregano, salt, and pepper in a large bowl. Toss potatoes in the mixture. Transfer to 13 x 9-inch baking dish and bake, uncovered, for 30 minutes or until soft.

Makes 6 servings

PER SERVING: calories 141, protein: 3 g, carbohydrate: 28 g, fat: 2 g, dietary fiber: 3 g, sodium: 200 mg

EXCELLENT SOURCE OF: vitamins B₆ and C (Yes! Even roasted.)
GOOD SOURCE OF: potassium, niacin, thiamin

% CALORIES FROM: protein 7%, fat 15%, carbohydrate 78%

Mashed Potatoes with Coriander

Few foods are as comforting as creamy mashed potatoes. Fresh herbs and spices, such as the coriander in this recipe, can add interesting flavor combinations. As in the Dijon Scalloped Potatoes (page 170) and the Potato Dill Salad (page 97), skins are left on for added nutritional value.

4 potatoes (unpeeled)	1/2 teaspoon coriander seeds,
1/2 cup soy or dairy milk	crushed
2 tablespoons chopped fresh	1/4 teaspoon salt
parsley	Pinch pepper
1 tablespoon extra-virgin olive	1 tablespoon chopped green
oil (optional)	onions

Quarter potatoes and cook in pot of boiling water for 15 to 20 minutes or until tender. Drain water from pot and reserve for vegetable stock. Add milk, parsley, olive oil (if using), coriander, salt, and pepper, and mash well by hand or with an electric beater. Blend in green onions and adjust seasoning.

VARIATIONS: Add one of the following to the above recipe:
- ◆ 1/4 cup Pesto-the Best-Oh! (page 80)
- ◆ 1/4 cup sun-dried tomatoes, soaked in water, drained, and diced
- ◆ 2–3 cloves roasted garlic, puréed
- ◆ fresh cracked pepper to taste
- ◆ 1–2 tablespoons chopped fresh herbs such as basil, thyme, oregano, or cilantro

Makes 4 servings

PER SERVING: calories 129, protein: 3 g, carbohydrate: 29 g, fat: 0.6 g, dietary fiber: 3 g, sodium: 173 mg
WITH OIL: calories 161, fat 4 g.

EXCELLENT SOURCE OF: vitamins B6 and C
GOOD SOURCE OF: potassium, niacin, thiamin

% CALORIES FROM: protein 10%, fat 4%, carbohydrate 86%
WITH OIL: % CALORIES FROM: protein 8%, fat 22%, carbohydrate 70%

Mexican Rice

 This rice turns out very moist due to the addition of tomatoes, and the peppers, herbs, and spices provide a rich flavor. It is a great accompaniment to the Savory Black Bean Stew (page 147) or the Chili with Textured Soy Protein (page 131).

2 cups vegetable stock or
   2 teaspoons canola oil

1/2 small onion, diced

1 clove garlic, minced

2 cups chopped fresh or canned
   tomatoes (drained)

1 cup brown rice

1/4 cup diced sweet red pepper

1/4 cup diced green pepper

1/2 teaspoon dried oregano

1/2 teaspoon ground cumin

1/2 teaspoon chili powder

1/4 teaspoon salt

Pinch pepper

In pot, sauté onions and garlic in 2 tablespoons of the stock, adding more stock if necessary, or 2 teaspoons oil over medium heat for 5 minutes or until onion is soft. Add remaining stock, tomatoes, rice, red and green peppers, oregano, cumin, chili powder, salt, and pepper. Cover, reduce heat, and cook for 45 minutes.

Makes 4 servings

PER SERVING: calories 202, protein: 5 g, carbohydrate: 42 g, fat: 2 g, dietary fiber: 3 g, sodium: 152 mg
WITH OIL: calories: 222, fat 4 g

EXCELLENT SOURCE OF: magnesium, vitamin C
GOOD SOURCE OF: potassium, niacin, thiamin, vitamin B6

% CALORIES FROM: protein 9%, fat 8%, carbohydrate 83%
WITH OIL: % CALORIES FROM: protein 9%, fat 16%, carbohydrate 75%

Potato Subji

India has a tradition of vegetarian cuisine with roots in antiquity. As a consequence, its food combinations have a great deal to offer the West in depth, color, richness, and variety. An example is found here in one of the tastiest ways ever created to eat potatoes!

2 tablespoons canola oil

1 tablespoon mustard seeds

1 onion, diced

2 teaspoons turmeric

4 potatoes cut in 1/2-inch cubes

1 teaspoon salt

1/4 cup water (more if necessary)

Heat mustard seeds in oil over medium heat in pan. Once seeds begin to pop, cover pan with lid and wait until they've all popped, about 1 1/2 minutes. Add onion and turmeric; sauté for 3 to 5 minutes or until onion is soft. Stir in potatoes, salt, and water. Cover and simmer for 20 minutes or until potatoes are tender, adding more water if necessary to prevent potatoes from drying out.

Makes 4 servings

PER SERVING: 188 calories, protein: 4 g, carbohydrate: 27 g, fat: 8 g, dietary fiber: 3 g, sodium: 591 mg

EXCELLENT SOURCE OF: vitamin C
GOOD SOURCE OF: iron, magnesium, niacin, vitamin B$_6$

% CALORIES FROM: protein 8%, fat 37%, carbohydrate 55%

Red Cabbage with Walnuts

 Here's a dish bursting with health! The brassica (cabbage) family contains valuable phytochemicals that help protect us against cancer. The oils in walnuts are rich in essential omega-3 fatty acids. The sweet, smooth taste of balsamic vinegar comes from being aged in wooden casks for up to 10 years.

1/4 head red cabbage, thinly
    sliced (4 cups)
2 tablespoons water
1/2 cup chopped walnuts

2 tablespoons balsamic vinegar
1–2 teaspoons extra-virgin olive
    oil (optional)
1/2 teaspoon tamari or soy sauce

In covered pan over medium heat, sauté cabbage in water for 5 to 8 minutes or until the cabbage is wilted. Stir in walnuts, vinegar, oil (if using), and tamari; cook for 2 to 3 minutes.

Makes 4 servings.

PER SERVING: calories 122, protein: 3 g, carbohydrate: 9 g,
fat: 9 g, dietary fiber: 3 g, sodium: 53 mg
WITH OIL: calories 132, fat 11 g

EXCELLENT SOURCE OF: vitamin C, omega-3 fatty acids
GOOD SOURCE OF: vitamin B6

% CALORIES FROM: protein 10%, fat 64%, carbohydrate 26%
WITH OIL: % CALORIES FROM: protein 9%, fat 67%, carbohydrate 24%

Roasted Root Vegetables

 Root vegetables are a part of the autumn harvest that provides a great deal of nourishment and warmth. We have chosen a combination particularly rich in vitamin A, however, you may want to include other vegetables such as parsnips, turnips, and squash.

2 carrots

2 yams

2 potatoes

1 large onion

2 tablespoons extra-virgin
  olive oil

1 tablespoon chopped fresh herbs
  (such as basil, thyme, oregano,
  dill) or 1 teaspoon dried herbs

1/4 teaspoon salt

Pinch pepper

Preheat oven to 375°. Cut vegetables into 2-inch pieces and place them in large bowl. Sprinkle with oil, herbs, salt, and pepper, tossing well to coat vegetables. Transfer to 13 x 9-inch baking dish. Bake, uncovered, for 35 to 40 minutes or until vegetables are tender.

Makes 4 servings

PER SERVING: calories 287, protein: 5 g, carbohydrate: 53 g, fat: 7 g, dietary fiber: 8 g, sodium: 212 mg

EXCELLENT SOURCE OF: potassium, vitamins A, B₆, and C
GOOD SOURCE OF: iron, magnesium, folate, niacin, riboflavin, thiamin

% CALORIES FROM: protein 6%, fat 22%, carbohydrate 72%

Seasoned Potato Wedges

 These potatoes are a delicious alternative to French fries. Easy to prepare, they can be served alone or with Spicy Peanut Sauce (page 190), Cucumber Dill Dressing (page 104), barbecue sauce, or other favorite dipping sauces. Experiment with different herb and spice combinations in the yeast mixture. Any leftover yeast can be sprinkled over casseroles, salad, or popcorn.

4 Russet potatoes

1/4–1/3 cup plain soy, rice, or
   dairy milk

1/2 teaspoon salt

1/3 cup nutritional yeast (page 218)

2 teaspoons onion powder

2 teaspoons chili powder

3/4 teaspoon garlic powder

1/4 teaspoon pepper

Preheat oven to 400°. Cut each potato in half lengthwise; cut each half into thirds. Pour milk and salt into flat-bottomed bowl and stir to dissolve salt. Sprinkle yeast onto a plate; stir in onion, chili, and garlic powders, and pepper. Dip potatoes into milk then into yeast mixture until coated on all surfaces. Arrange on nonstick baking sheet and bake for 30 minutes.

VARIATION: For crispy wedges, lightly oil a baking sheet and arrange potatoes cut side down. Bake in 400° oven for 15 minutes. Using fork or metal tongs, turn wedges and bake for another 15 minutes.

Makes 24 wedges

PER ONE-QUARTER RECIPE/SIX WEDGES: calories 171, protein: 8 g, carbohydrate: 36g, fat: 1 g, dietary fiber: 4 g, sodium: 318 mg

EXCELLENT SOURCE OF: potassium, folate, niacin, riboflavin, thiamin, vitamins B_6, B_{12}, and C
GOOD SOURCE OF: iron, magnesium, zinc

% CALORIES FROM: protein 17%, fat 5%, carbohydrate 78%

(Note that in French fries, more than a third of the calories come from fat.)

Red Star Vegetarian Support Formula nutritional yeast provides vitamin B_{12}

Spaghetti Squash

Spaghetti squash resembles spaghetti when it is cooked and scooped out of the skin with a fork. Many people do not know how to use it, so here is an easy recipe that combines fresh tomatoes and basil as part of a simple summer meal.

1 spaghetti squash

1/4 cup chopped fresh or canned tomatoes (drained)

1/2 teaspoon extra-virgin olive oil (optional)

1–2 teaspoons chopped fresh herbs such as basil, thyme, or parsley

Salt and pepper

Preheat oven to 375°. Cut squash in half lengthwise. Scoop out seeds. Lay cut side of squash down on a baking pan. Add 1/2 cup of water to pan and bake for 30 minutes or until indentation remains in skin of squash when pressed. Remove from oven and turn squash over to let steam escape and prevent steam from overcooking squash. Once squash is cool enough to handle, scoop out pulp into bowl using fork or spoon. Stir in tomatoes, olive oil (if using), herbs, salt, and pepper. Transfer to pan, cover, and heat over medium heat for 3 to 5 minutes.

Makes 4 servings

PER SERVING: calories 27, protein: 0.7 g, carbohydrate: 6 g, fat: 0.3 g, dietary fiber: 1 g, sodium: 16 mg WITH OIL: Calories 32, Fat 0.8 g

GOOD SOURCE OF: vitamin C

% CALORIES FROM: protein 10%, fat 8%, carbohydrate 82%
WITH OIL: % CALORIES FROM: protein 8%, fat 22%, carbohydrate 70%

Spinach with Garam Masala

Garam masala *means warm mixture in Hindi. It is composed of cinnamon, clove, nutmeg, cardamom, mace, and black pepper—a combination of spices that has a warming effect on the body. In this modification of a classic Indian dish, small white cubes of tofu rest on a sea of delicately seasoned and puréed green spinach.*

2 bunches fresh spinach (6 cups)
1 small onion, diced
2 teaspoons canola oil
3/4 teaspoon garam masala
1/2 teaspoon ground coriander

1/4 teaspoon garlic powder
1/4 teaspoon salt
1/2 teaspoon lemon juice
1/4 cup finely diced firm tofu

Preheat oven to 325°. Wash spinach well. Steam over medium-high heat for about 3 minutes or until wilted. Meanwhile, sauté onions over medium heat in oil for 3 to 5 minutes or until soft. Stir in garam masala, coriander, garlic powder, and salt; sauté for 2 to 3 minutes, stirring frequently to prevent spices from sticking.

In food processor, purée cooked spinach, onion mixture, and lemon juice until smooth. Transfer to ovenproof dish, stir in tofu, and heat in oven for 10 minutes or until tofu is warmed through.

VARIATION: Substitute 6 cups kale for spinach in the above dish. Add 3 tablespoons kale cooking liquid to food processor. The product will have a more fibrous texture than spinach and the added benefit of 550 milligrams of highly absorbable calcium per cup! (Makes 1 cup).

Makes 4 servings

PER SERVING: calories 71, protein: 5 g, carbohydrate: 6 g, fat: 4 g, dietary fiber: 3 g, sodium: 211 mg

EXCELLENT SOURCE OF: iron, magnesium, folate, vitamin A
GOOD SOURCE OF: riboflavin, vitamins B6 and C

% CALORIES FROM: protein 27%, fat 44%, carbohydrate 29%

Spinach with Gomasio

 The next time you go to a Japanese restaurant, order Spinach Gomae along with vegetarian sushi and perhaps a tofu dish. In the meantime, here is our version of this warm spinach salad that you can make at home.

2 bunches torn fresh spinach
  (6 cups)
2 teaspoons flaxseed oil or
  canola oil

2 teaspoons lemon juice
1 teaspoon tamari or soy sauce
1 teaspoon Gomasio (page 76
  or commercial)

Wash spinach well and remove stems. Steam spinach in steamer over medium-high heat for 3 minutes or until leaves are just wilted. Mix oil, lemon juice, and tamari in a bowl. Stir in steamed spinach and toss. Sprinkle with Gomasio.

Makes 4 servings

PER SERVING: calories 48, protein: 3 g, carbohydrate: 4 g, fat: 3 g, dietary fiber: 2 g, sodium: 159 mg

EXCELLENT SOURCE OF: magnesium, folate, vitamin A, omega-3 fatty acids
GOOD SOURCE OF: potassium, riboflavin, vitamins B$_6$ and C

% CALORIES FROM: protein 22%, fat 49%, carbohydrate 29%

Zucchini, Onion, and Tomato

 Here's another simple vegetable recipe that can be made in minutes during the summer months when zucchini is so abundant in your garden, or inexpensive at the farmers' market or supermarket. It provides a good example of the oil-free style of cooking that is found throughout the book. For a description of the cooking method, see page 48.

2 cups fresh or canned tomatoes

1 onion, chopped

1 clove minced garlic

2 cups diced zucchini

1 tablespoon chopped fresh basil

  (or 1 teaspoon dried basil)

1/4 teaspoon salt

Pinch pepper

In pan, sauté tomatoes, onion, and garlic over medium heat for 3 to 5 minutes. Stir in zucchini, basil, salt, and pepper; cook for 5 minutes or until zucchini is soft. Adjust seasoning.

Makes 4 servings

PER SERVING: calories: 82, protein: 3 g, carbohydrate: 19 g, fat: 1 g, dietary fiber: 4 g, sodium: 200 mg

EXCELLENT SOURCE OF: potassium, vitamin C
GOOD SOURCE OF: magnesium, folate, thiamin, vitamins A and B6

% CALORIES FROM: protein 13%, fat 8%, carbohydrate 79%

Sauces

Blueberry Orange Sauce

This easy-to-make sauce is a treat on pancakes, Vegan Dass Ice Cream (page 216) or Lem-Un-Cheesecake (page 212).

2 cups blueberries, fresh or frozen

1 cup apple juice

1/4 cup maple syrup, Sucanat (page 219), or honey

1/2 teaspoon cinnamon

3/4 cup orange juice concentrate

2–3 tablespoons cornstarch or arrowroot

Heat blueberries, apple juice, maple syrup, and cinnamon in saucepan over medium heat until berries are cooked into mash, about 10 minutes. Combine orange juice concentrate and cornstarch in measuring cup. Stir cornstarch mixture into berry mixture. Bring to boil; simmer 2 to 3 minutes until thickened.

Makes 1 3/4 cups

PER 1/4-CUP SERVING: calories 127, protein: 1 g, carbohydrate: 31 g, fat: 0.4 g, dietary fiber: 2 g, sodium: 4 mg

EXCELLENT SOURCE OF: vitamin C
GOOD SOURCE OF: folate

% CALORIES FROM: protein 3%, fat 3%, carbohydrate 94%

Cranberry Ginger Relish

 Cranberry relish can evoke wonderful memories of Thanksgiving and Christmas. Serve it as a side dish with Stuffed Winter Squash (page 149) and Light Mushroom Gravy (page 188) or Rosemary Gravy (page 189).

1/2 cup red currant jelly or
   apple jelly

1/4 cup finely diced red onion

12-ounce bag fresh or frozen
   cranberries

2 tablespoons orange juice
   concentrate

1/2 teaspoon ground ginger

1/4 teaspoon ground cinnamon

1/4 teaspoon salt

2–4 tablespoons Sucanat (page
   219), or brown sugar

Heat jelly and onion in pan over medium heat until jelly melts, about 5 minutes. Place cranberries in food processor and, using pulse action, chop berries but don't purée them. Scrape down sides and pulse for 2 seconds more. Add berries to jelly along with orange juice, ginger, cinnamon, and salt. Reduce heat and simmer, uncovered, for 10 minutes. Stir occasionally. Stir in Sucanat.

Makes 2 cups

PER 1/4-CUP SERVING: calories 84, protein: 0.4 g, carbohydrate: 22 g, fat: 0.1 g, dietary fiber: 2 g, sodium: 81 mg

% CALORIES FROM: protein 2%, fat 1%, carbohydrate 97%

Light Mushroom Gravy

 This recipe is ideal with Stuffed Winter Squash (page 149), but it can also be served with baked or mashed potatoes or with veggie burgers. The no-added-oil approach allows you to use as much gravy as you want—in good health! If you use stock cubes or powder, experiment with different brands, as flavorful stock makes a big difference. Stocks vary in saltiness, so adjust the amount of tamari accordingly. Double the recipe to use for leftovers.

3 cups vegetable stock

1 cup thinly sliced mushrooms

1/2 cup diced onion

1/4 cup diced carrot

1/4 cup diced celery

2 cloves garlic, chopped

2–3 tablespoons tamari or
   soy sauce

2 tablespoons chopped parsley

1 tablespoon nutritional yeast
   (page 218)

1/4 teaspoon dried thyme

1/4 teaspoon dried sage

1/2 cup unbleached or
   all-purpose flour

3/4 cup water

Salt and pepper

Sauté mushrooms, onion, carrot, celery, and garlic in 2 tablespoons of the stock, adding more stock if necessary, in pan over medium heat for 5 minutes or until onion is soft. Stir in remaining stock, tamari, parsley, yeast, thyme, and sage. Measure flour and water into a jar, cover tightly with lid, and shake until blended. Strain mixture into pan. Bring to boil, reduce heat, and simmer, uncovered, for 15 to 20 minutes. Stir frequently. Adjust seasoning.

NOTE: If gravy is too thick, add more stock. If gravy is too thin, simmer uncovered to let moisture evaporate.

Makes 4 cups

PER 1/4-CUP SERVING: calories 25, protein: 1 g, carbohydrate: 5 g, fat: 0.1 g, dietary fiber: 0.6 g, sodium: 132 mg

GOOD SOURCE OF: niacin riboflavin, thiamin, vitamin B6

% CALORIES FROM: protein 19%, fat 5%, carbohydrate 76%

Rosemary Gravy

Can gravy taste good when made without the drippings? Yes! You'll find that the familiar Thanksgiving seasonings of rosemary, thyme, and sage make this gravy just as much a part of festive seasons as any gravy you've had before.

1/2 cup canola oil

1/4 cup diced onion

1/4 cup diced carrot

1/4 cup diced celery

2 cloves garlic, chopped

1/2 cup unbleached or all-purpose white flour

3 cups vegetable stock

2–3 tablespoons tamari or soy sauce

2 tablespoons chopped fresh parsley

2 teaspoons dried rosemary

1 teaspoon dried thyme

1/2 teaspoon dried sage

1/4 teaspoon pepper

Salt

Sauté onion, carrot, celery, and garlic in canola oil in pan over medium heat for 5 minutes. Stir in flour to absorb the oil and cook for another 5 minutes, stirring frequently. Remove pot from heat for 3 minutes to cool. (If you add stock to hot mix, flour will lump.) Return to heat after 2 to 3 minutes and gradually pour in stock. Stir constantly, allowing flour to absorb liquid before adding more stock. Continue until stock is used up. Add tamari, parsley, rosemary, thyme, sage, and pepper. Bring to boil, reduce heat, and simmer, uncovered, for 15 to 20 minutes. Stir frequently. Adjust seasoning.

NOTE: If gravy is too thick, add more stock. If gravy is too thin, simmer, uncovered, to let moisture evaporate.

Makes 3 1/2 cups

PER 1/4-CUP SERVING: calories 91, protein: 0.9 g, carbohydrate: 5 g, fat: 8 g, dietary fiber: 0.5 g, sodium: 150 mg

% CALORIES FROM: protein 4%, fat 76%, carbohydrate 20%

Spicy Peanut Sauce

 This recipe can be used as a dipping sauce for Fresh Vegetable Salad Roll (page 95). Use it as a sauce with broccoli and other vegetables, served over hot rice, or with Thai Pasta Salad (page 100). This sauce keeps well in the refrigerator for up to 2 weeks. If it thickens after sitting in the refrigerator, simply thin with warm water to desired consistency.

4-inch piece gingerroot, peeled and chopped (1/3 cup)

6 cloves garlic

1 bunch cilantro leaves, chopped

1/2 cup unsweetened, unsalted peanut butter

1/2 cup tamari or soy sauce

2 tablespoons Sucanat (page 219) or brown sugar

2 tablespoons rice vinegar or cider vinegar

2 teaspoons toasted sesame oil

1/2 teaspoon chopped fresh chili pepper

In food processor, combine gingerroot, garlic, cilantro, peanut butter, tamari, Sucanat, vinegar, sesame oil, and chili. Process until smooth. Sauce should slightly pour; if it doesn't, add small amount of hot water until it flows.

Makes 1 3/4 cups

PER 2 TABLESPOONS: calories 69, protein: 3 g, carbohydrate: 3 g, fat: 5 g, dietary fiber: 0.8 g, sodium: 576 mg

% CALORIES FROM: protein 18%, fat 64%, carbohydrate 18%

Tamarind Date Sauce

 Tamarind is an Indian fruit that grows in a pod. This sauce, made from a concentrate of the fruit, adds unique lemony sharpness when served as a condiment with Potato Subji (page 177), Seasoned Potato Wedges (page 180), curries, or in an Indonesian Roll-Up (page 139). Tamarind paste can be purchased at East Indian groceries. While you're there, enjoy the aromas of exotic ingredients and stock up on papadums, almonds, and spices such as curry paste and curry powder, garam masala, and cumin.

3/4 cup hot water

3/4 cup chopped pitted dates

3 tablespoons tamarind paste

2 tablespoons apple cider vinegar

1 tablespoon minced, peeled
  gingerroot

2 teaspoons orange juice
  concentrate

1/2 teaspoon garam masala

Pinch salt

Pour water over dates and let sit for 30 minutes. Place dates with soaking water, tamarind paste, vinegar, ginger, orange juice concentrate, garam masala, and salt in food processor and blend until smooth, occasionally scraping down sides of bowl. (This sauce can be kept refrigerated for several weeks.)

Makes 1 1/4 cups

PER TABLESPOON: calories 21, protein: 0.2 g, carbohydrate: 6 g, fat: 0.1 g, dietary fiber: 0.6 g, sodium: 10 mg

% CALORIES FROM: protein 3%, fat 2%, carbohydrate 95%

Teriyaki Sauce

 Teriyaki sauce is common in Japanese cuisine. It adds both sweet and salty flavors to the food with which it is blended. The first choice for this recipe is sake, a Japanese rice wine that has a clean but distinctive taste and adds a lot of character. If you prefer not to use alcohol in your cooking, the sake can be replaced with stock, preferably a no-salt version. Mirin is a sweet cooking seasoning found in Japanese markets and natural food stores. Teriyaki sauce can be added to stir-fries, tofu, or rice.

1/2 cup light or regular tamari
  or soy sauce

1/2 cup sake or vegetable stock

1/2 cup mirin

1/2 cup packed brown sugar

1/2 onion, chopped

3 tablespoons thinly sliced
  gingerroot (unpeeled)

4 cloves garlic, chopped

1 tablespoon cornstarch

1 tablespoon water

Bring tamari, sake, mirin, brown sugar, onion, ginger, and garlic to boil in pan over high heat. Immediately reduce heat and simmer for 10 minutes. Dissolve cornstarch in water and stir into pan. Cook, stirring, until thickened. After sauce thickens, simmer for 3 minutes, then strain. The sauce keeps in the refrigerator for several weeks.

Makes 2 cups

PER TABLESPOON: calories 33, protein: 0.5 g, carbohydrate: 6 g, fat: 0, dietary fiber: 0, sodium: 128 mg*

% CALORIES FROM: protein 6%, fat 0, carbohydrate 71% alcohol 23%
WITH STOCK: carbohydrate 94%, alcohol 0%

*Analyzed using light soy sauce

Tomato-Miso Sauce

Miso gives this sauce robust flavor. If you're serving this sauce with noodles, you'll need 2 to 3 ounces of noodles per person. An easy way to gauge this is to grasp a bunch of dry noodles the size of a quarter for each adult, or more for a very hungry adult.

2 tablespoons water or
  1 tablespoon extra-virgin olive
  oil
1/2 onion, diced
1/2 cup diced carrot
1/2 cup diced celery
1/4 cup diced sweet red pepper
2 cloves garlic, chopped
3 cups chopped fresh or
  canned tomatoes (28 ounces)

5-ounce can tomato paste
1 teaspoon dried basil
1/2 teaspoon dried oregano
1/8 teaspoon black pepper
2 tablespoons miso
2 tablespoons water
2 tablespoons Sucanat (page 219)
  or brown sugar
1/4 teaspoon salt (optional)

In pan over medium heat, sauté onion, carrot, celery, pepper, and garlic in 2 tablespoons water, adding more water if necessary, or in 1 tablespoon oil for 5 minutes. Stir in tomatoes, tomato paste, basil, oregano, and pepper; cover, reduce heat, and simmer for 20 minutes. Mix together miso and water to form a paste; stir into sauce along with Sucanat. Heat through and adjust seasoning.

Makes about five 1-cup servings

PER SERVING: calories 100, protein: 4 g, carbohydrate: 21 g, fat: 1g, dietary fiber: 4 g, sodium: 517 mg

EXCELLENT SOURCE OF: potassium, vitamins A and C
GOOD SOURCE OF: iron, magnesium, niacin, riboflavin, thiamin, vitamins B_6 and E

% CALORIES FROM: protein 14%, fat 10%, carbohydrate 76%

Tomato Sauce Variations

 If you're cooking for one or two people, here are three easy ways to add protein and the trace minerals calcium, iron, and zinc to a cup of your favorite commercial tomato sauce (or to the Tomato-Miso Sauce recipe on page 193). Serve these sauces with noodles or veggie patties, or in any other way that you normally use tomato sauce.

Tomato Sauce with Aduki Beans

In Japan, aduki (also called adzuki) beans have a reputation as an excellent source of dietary iron. In fact, when a Japanese girl has her first menstrual period, the family will often honor the occasion by serving a dish of red beans and rice, called Sekihan, that replenishes her iron! The small red aduki beans can be cooked in 60 minutes after soaking, or in 90 minutes without soaking (see legumes chart in appendix, page 226). Cooked beans freeze well, so keep a few portions in the freezer in plastic containers for instant use.

I cup tomato sauce

3/4 cup cooked or canned aduki beans, mashed

Heat tomato sauce and beans.

Makes 1 3/4 cups

PER RECIPE: calories 300, fat 0.6 g, protein: 16 g, calcium 100 mg, iron 5.9 mg, zinc 3.3 mg

% CALORIES FROM: protein 20%, fat 2%, carbohydrate 78%

Tomato Sauce with Textured Soy Protein
(Happy Camper's Tomato Sauce)

Textured soy protein, also known as textured vegetable protein or TVP, is a simple way to add protein and minerals to tomato sauce, soups, and casseroles without added fat. Since it is dehydrated, it is extremely light and has a long shelf life, so it's handy for backpacking and camping trips.

1 cup tomato sauce	2 tablespoons textured soy protein

Heat tomato sauce, add textured soy protein, and simmer 15 minutes.

Makes 1 1/8 cups

PER RECIPE: calories 108, fat 0.6 g, protein: 9 g, calcium 85 mg, iron 3.5 mg, zinc 0.8 mg

% CALORIES FROM: protein 27%, fat 4%, carbohydrate 69%

Tomato Sauce with Tofu

Here is yet another use for this very versatile product—tofu can be mashed into tomato sauce and used with all sorts of pasta dishes. Instead, you may prefer to purée the mixture in a blender.

1 cup tomato sauce	1/2 cup firm tofu

Mash tofu and add tomato sauce or combine in a blender; heat in saucepan.

Makes 1 1/2 cups

PER RECIPE: calories 174, fat 6 g, protein: 14 g, calcium: 485 mg, iron 9 mg, zinc 1.2 mg

% CALORIES FROM: protein 27%, fat 28%, carbohydrate 45%

FOR COMPARISON: PER CUP MUIR GLEN ORGANIC TOMATO SAUCE: calories 79, fat 0.4 g protein: 4 g, calcium 51 mg, iron 2.48 mg, zinc 0.3 mg

% Calories from: protein 14%, fat 4%, carbohydrate 82%

Desserts

Apple Cranberry Kanten

 A traditional Japanese fruit dessert, kanten is a very simple dish that is easy to prepare. Serve it chilled after a heavier meal or on a hot summer evening.

2 cups apple juice

2 cups sweetened cranberry juice

1/8 teaspoon ground cinnamon

1/8 teaspoon ground nutmeg

Pinch ground allspice

Pinch ground cloves

Pinch salt

1/3 cup agar flakes or 2 teaspoons agar powder (see page 217)

1 cup firm, fresh fruit such as blueberries, diced cantaloupe, or sliced banana

Place fruit juices, cinnamon, nutmeg, allspice, cloves, and salt into pot. Bring to boil over medium heat. Immediately reduce heat to low. Stir in agar and cook, stirring occasionally, for 5 minutes or until agar dissolves. Pour into serving bowl and refrigerate for 4 to 5 hours or until set. Just before serving, stir with whisk and fold in fruit.

VARIATION: This dish can be made with one fruit juice or the other.

Makes 4 servings

PER SERVING: calories 155, protein: 0.4 g, carbohydrate: 39 g, fat: 0.4 g, dietary fiber: 1.4 g, sodium: 10 mg

EXCELLENT SOURCE OF: vitamin C

% CALORIES FROM: protein 1%, fat 2%, carbohydrate 97%

Apple Pear Crumble

 Many other fruits can be substituted for apples and pears in this recipe. Try peaches or nectarines with blueberries or raspberries and use a total of 7 to 8 cups of fruit.

3 unpeeled apples, cored and chopped

3 unpeeled pears, cored and chopped

2 tablespoons lemon juice

3 tablespoons maple syrup

1/4 cup raisins

Preheat oven to 350°. Toss lemon juice with fruit in 8-inch baking dish. Drizzle maple syrup and sprinkle raisins over top.

Topping

2 cups rolled oats

1/4 cup chopped walnuts

1/2 cup orange juice concentrate

1/3 cup water

3 tablespoons maple syrup

1 1/2 teaspoons whole-wheat flour

1/2 teaspoon ground cinnamon

1/8 teaspoon nutmeg

In bowl combine oats, walnuts, orange juice concentrate, water, maple syrup, flour, cinnamon, and nutmeg. Let mixture sit for 10 minutes for oats to absorb liquid. Spread mixture evenly over fruit and bake for 25 to 30 minutes or until golden brown.

VARIATION: Substitute 1 cup of apples or pears with 1 cup of cranberries.

Makes 6 servings

PER SERVING: calories 338, protein: 6 g, carbohydrate: 70 g, fat: 6 g, dietary fiber: 8 g, sodium: 6 mg
WITHOUT WALNUTS: calories 306, fat 2 g

EXCELLENT SOURCE OF: thiamin
GOOD SOURCE OF: iron, magnesium, potassium, folate

% CALORIES FROM: protein 7%, fat 14%, carbohydrate 79%
WITHOUT WALNUTS: % CALORIES FROM: protein 7%, fat 7%, carbohydrate 86%

Apple Spice Cake

 This lovely cake can be used as a family dessert or for a festive occasion like a wedding or birthday. Serve it plain or with your favorite icing.

3 cups whole-wheat pastry flour

1 tablespoon baking powder

2 teaspoons ground cinnamon

1 teaspoon baking soda

1 teaspoon ground cloves

1 teaspoon ground allspice

1 teaspoon ground nutmeg

1 teaspoon ground ginger

1/2 teaspoon salt

1 cup maple syrup, honey, or
    corn syrup

1 cup soy or dairy milk

2/3 cup canola oil

2 tablespoons ground flaxseed
    (see page 218) or 2 eggs

2 cups grated apples

1 cup raisins

1 cup chopped walnuts or pecans

Preheat oven to 350°. In bowl, mix flour, baking powder, cinnamon, baking soda, cloves, allspice, nutmeg, ginger, and salt. In large bowl, combine maple syrup, milk, oil, and flaxseed. Stir flour mixture into wet ingredients until blended. Fold in apples, raisins, and nuts. Do not over-mix. Pour into oiled and floured 13 x 9-inch baking pan. Bake for 35 to 40 minutes or until a toothpick inserted into cake comes out clean.

Makes 24 pieces.

PER PIECE: calories 208, protein: 3 g, carbohydrate: 29 g, fat: 10 g, dietary fiber: 3 g, sodium: 157 mg

% CALORIES FROM: protein 6%, fat 41%, carbohydrate 53%

Analyzed using ProSoya So Nice original soy beverage

Baked Stuffed Apples

This recipe is equally tasty made with Macintosh apples, which are quick to cook, or other varieties such as Golden Delicious or Granny Smith, which may take longer.

4 baking apples	2 teaspoons maple syrup, Sucanat
4 cup tahini	(page 219) or brown sugar
1/4 cup raisins	1/4 teaspoon ground cinnamon
2 teaspoons lemon juice	Pinch ground cardamom (optional)
1/2 teaspoon grated lemon rind	1/2 cup orange juice

Preheat oven to 300°. Pierce top of apple holding paring knife at a 45 degree angle to stem. Rotate knife around top to produce small cone-shaped top. Set tops aside. Using a melon baller or teaspoon, remove core from apples, being careful not to pierce the bottom of apples.

In small bowl, stir together tahini, raisins, lemon juice, rind, maple syrup, cinnamon, and cardamom (if using). Fill apple cavities almost to top with raisin mixture. Replace apple tops. Set apples in baking tray, pour orange juice over apples and bake for 15 minutes or until apples are soft when pierced with toothpick.

VARIATION: Replace tahini with 3 figs that have been soaked overnight, stems removed, and chopped.

Makes 4 servings

PER APPLE: calories 246, protein: 4 g, carbohydrate: 43 g, fat: 9 g, dietary fiber: 6 g, sodium: 2 mg

EXCELLENT SOURCE OF: thiamin
GOOD SOURCE OF: magnesium, potassium, zinc

% CALORIES FROM: protein 5%, fat 31%, carbohydrate 64%

Blueberry Corn Muffins

 What better choice for brunch, afternoon tea, or an evening get-together than muffins that are both delicious and healthy too! These muffins are cholesterol-free, lactose-free, and packed with good nutrition. You can use a combination of unbleached or all-purpose flour and whole wheat pastry flour, as shown below, or use entirely one flour or the other. If you prefer, you may replace the ground flaxseed with an egg.

I cup whole-wheat pastry flour

I cup unbleached or all-purpose flour

I 1/2 teaspoons baking powder

1/2 teaspoon baking soda

1/2 teaspoon salt

I cup cornmeal

2/3 cup Sucanat (page 219) or brown sugar

I 1/2 cups soy or dairy milk

1/3 cup canola oil

I 1/2 cups blueberries, fresh or frozen

Preheat oven to 400°. In small bowl, mix flours, baking powder, soda, and salt. In large bowl, combine cornmeal, Sucanat, soy milk, and oil and let sit for 3 minutes. Stir flour into wet mixture and stir just until blended. Do not overmix. Fold in blueberries. Spoon into lightly oiled muffin tins and bake for 25 to 30 minutes or until golden brown. If using frozen blueberries, you will probably need the longer baking time.

Makes 12 muffins

PER MUFFIN: calories 159, protein: 3 g, carbohydrate: 21 g, fat: 7 g, dietary fiber: 3 g, sodium: 232 mg

% CALORIES FROM: protein 8%, fat 40%, carbohydrate 51%

Analyzed using ProSoya So Nice original soy beverage

Blueberry Mince Tarts

Blueberries and cranberries, two of the most delicious fruit crops of the Pacific Northwest, are combined in this mouth-watering tart filling. With all the heavy foods around during the holiday season, these tarts are refreshingly light.

Blueberry Filling

1 1/4 cups sultana raisins

1 1/4 cups golden raisins

1/2 cup dried cranberries

1/2 cup Sucanat (page 219) or
   brown sugar

1/3 cup mixed candied peel

2 tablespoons fruit juice or brandy

1 tablespoon lemon juice

1 teaspoon grated lemon rind

1 teaspoon ground cinnamon

1/2 teaspoon ground cloves

1/2 teaspoon ground ginger

1/2 teaspoon ground nutmeg

4 cups fresh or frozen blueberries

Combine raisins, cranberries, Sucanat, mixed peel, fruit juice, lemon juice, rind, cinnamon, cloves, ginger, and nutmeg in large bowl. Stir in blueberries.

Pastry

Rolling pastry is easy—no flour on the countertop to clean up afterwards—if you roll it between two clean plastic bags (cut down two sides and opened).

1/2 cup ice water

1 1/2 cups whole-wheat pastry
   flour

1 1/2 cups unbleached or
   all-purpose flour

1 tablespoon baking powder

1/2 teaspoon salt

1/2 cup safflower, sunflower, or
   corn oil

Let several ice cubes stand in glass of water to make ice water. Meanwhile, in bowl, stir flours, baking powder, and salt with whisk or fork until well mixed. Stir in oil, tossing mixture with fork until small balls form. Sprinkle ice water gradually into mixture, tossing with fork until all flour is incorporated. Gather into two balls.

To Assemble

Preheat oven to 400°. Roll out each ball between plastic bags or sheets of waxed paper the thickness of a nickel. To cut out tarts, use 4-inch diameter jar lid. Lift dough circles with pancake turner and place in lightly oiled or nonstick muffin tin.

Place slightly more than 1/4-cup blueberry filling into each tart shell. Bake for 17 to 20 minutes or until crust begins to brown. Cool before removing tarts from tins.

Leftover filling can be stored in refrigerator or freezer.

Makes 7 1/2 cups filling, 20 large tarts

PER FILLED TART: calories 211, protein: 3 g, carbohydrate: 39 g, fat: 6 g, dietary fiber: 3 g, sodium: 137 mg

% CALORIES FROM: protein 5%, fat 25%, carbohydrate 70%

Brown Rice Pudding

 Brown rice quickly becomes a mainstay and a favorite in a vegetarian's kitchen pantry. It provides a wider assortment of trace minerals and B vitamins than its refined counterpart, white rice. Cook rice in large batches and incorporate leftovers in this comforting dessert or in International Roll-Ups (page 139). This pudding also makes a fine breakfast food.

2 cups soy or dairy milk	2 teaspoons lemon juice
4 cups cooked brown rice	1 teaspoon vanilla extract
1/2 cup raisins or chopped dates	1/2 teaspoon ground cinnamon
1/4 cup maple syrup	1/8 teaspoon ground cloves
1/2 teaspoon grated lemon rind	1/8 teaspoon ground nutmeg

Preheat oven to 325°. Pour milk over rice in bowl. Stir in raisins, maple syrup, lemon rind and juice, vanilla, cinnamon, cloves, and nutmeg, mixing well. Pour into 8-inch square baking dish. Cover and bake for 30 to 40 minutes or until set.

Makes 5 servings

PER SERVING: calories 298, fat: 3 g, protein: 7 g, carbohydrate: 64 g, dietary fiber: 4 g, sodium: 73 mg

EXCELLENT SOURCE OF: magnesium
GOOD SOURCE OF: calcium*, iron, potassium, zinc, niacin, riboflavin, thiamin, vitamin B6

% CALORIES FROM: protein 8%, fat 8%, carbohydrate 84%

*Analyzed using ProSoya So Nice original soy beverage

Cashew Balls

These energy-packed balls are ideal for hiking trips, when space is at a premium. Eat one at the top of the mountain, and you'll have a peak experience!

1 cup cashew butter	1/4 teaspoon grated lemon rind
1/3 cup chopped, roasted, unsalted cashews	2 teaspoons lemon juice
1/4 cup currants	1/2 teaspoon vanilla extract
2 tablespoons tofu milk powder* or powdered milk	1/4 teaspoon ground cinnamon
1 tablespoon maple syrup or honey	1/4 teaspoon ground cardamom
	2 tablespoons finely shredded coconut

Combine cashew butter, cashews, currants, milk powder, maple syrup, lemon rind, juice, vanilla, cinnamon, and cardamom together in bowl. Roll 1 tablespoon of mixture between palms into a golf-ball size. Roll ball in coconut to coat.

Makes 10 balls

PER BALL: calories 208, protein: 6 g, carbohydrate: 15 g, fat: 15 g, dietary fiber: 1 g, sodium: 170 mg

EXCELLENT SOURCE OF: magnesium
GOOD SOURCE OF: iron, zinc

% CALORIES FROM: protein 10%, fat 63%, carbohydrate 26%

---

*Tofu milk powder, available at local health food stores, is a handy item to keep in your kitchen cupboard. It's easily mixed and can be used wherever soy or dairy milks are called for.

Chocolate Cream Couscous Cake

Executive Chef Ron Pickarski is a gold medalist at the International Culinary Olympics in Germany with his plant-based vegetarian displays. From his cookbook Friendly Foods *(published by Ten Speed Press), here's a simply delicious no-bake cake, representative of Pickarski's genius with foods. (Used with permission.)*

3/4 cup pecans

2 1/2 cups water

1 1/2 cups Sucanat (page 219)

1/4 cup cocoa powder

1 cup couscous

1 tablespoon vanilla extract

Preheat oven to 300°. Roast pecans for about 10 to 15 minutes. (Take care not to burn them.) Remove from oven and let cool. Grind in food processor for 5 to 10 seconds until consistency of coarse meal. Set aside. In saucepan, stir together water, Sucanat, cocoa, and couscous. Bring to simmer and cook until thickened, 5 to 10 minutes. Add vanilla and stir well. Spread mixture in 9-inch springform pan. Sprinkle 1/4 cup of the pecan meal over the couscous cake.

Filling

2 cups (12 ounces) chocolate chips, (barley malt or regular)

3 tablespoons maple syrup

2 packages (12 ounces each) firm silken tofu (at room temperature)

Melt chocolate chips in small saucepan over low heat, stirring constantly. Transfer to food processor. Add maple syrup and tofu, and blend until smooth. Pour filling over cake and top with remaining pecan meal. Refrigerate cake until set, about 2 hours. Serve cold.

VARIATION: This recipe also works well if you decrease the amount of Sucanat in the cake to 3/4 cup.

Makes 16 servings

PER SERVING: calories 220, protein: 6 g, carbohydrate: 29 g, fat: 11 g, dietary fiber: 2 g, sodium: 25 mg

GOOD SOURCE OF: magnesium

% CALORIES FROM: protein 10%, fat 41%, carbohydrate 49%

Cranberry Pecan Muffins

 These spectacular tasting muffins are the inspired creation of Brenda Davis, coauthor of Becoming Vegetarian *(published by The Book Publishing Company). The use of maple syrup offsets the tartness of the cranberries and provides a deep, sweet flavor. Stock your freezer with cranberries, as you'll want to make these muffins often.*

2 1/2 cups cranberries, fresh or frozen, thawed

1/2 cup maple syrup

1 teaspoon grated orange or lemon rind

1 1/2 cups soft tofu

1/3 cup canola oil

1/2 cup Sucanat (page 219) or packed brown sugar

1/2 cup soy or dairy milk

1 teaspoon vanilla extract

2 cups whole-wheat flour

2 teaspoons baking powder

2 teaspoons ground cinnamon

1 teaspoon baking soda

1/2 teaspoon cardamom

1/2 teaspoon allspice

1/2 teaspoon cloves

1/2 teaspoon salt

1 cup coarsely chopped pecans

Preheat oven to 375°. Cook 1 1/2 cups of cranberries with maple syrup and rind until berries have popped and liquid is thick. Chop remaining cranberries. Add to cooked berries and allow to cool while preparing muffin batter. Stir together tofu, canola oil, Sucanat, soy milk, and vanilla in large bowl. Mix flour, baking powder, cinnamon, baking soda, spices, and salt in small bowl. Add cranberries to wet ingredients. Mix well. Stir in dry ingredients along with pecans until just blended. Fill paper muffin cups and bake for 30 minutes or until an inserted toothpick comes out clean.

Makes 12 large muffins

PER MUFFIN: calories 260, protein: 5 g, carbohydrate: 31 g, fat: 14 g, dietary fiber: 4 g, sodium: 262 mg

GOOD SOURCE OF: calcium, iron, magnesium, zinc, thiamin

% CALORIES FROM: protein 8%, fat 47%, carbohydrate 45%

Figgy Pudding

 Figs have been gaining popularity now that we realize that 1/2 cup of figs contains as much calcium as 1/2 cup of milk. This recipe combines the goodness of apple juice, the smoothness of silken tofu, and the sweetness of figs. Serving in wide-mouthed champagne glasses adds an element of grace to this dessert.

I cup dried golden figs, stems
  removed (10–12 figs)

I 1/2 cups apple juice

12-ounce package firm silken tofu

I tablespoon lemon juice

I tablespoon Sucanat (page 219)
  or brown sugar

1/4 teaspoon ground cinnamon

1/4 teaspoon vanilla extract

Pinch ground cloves

I tablespoon slivered almonds
  (optional)

Soak figs in apple juice in refrigerator for 12 hours. Combine figs, apple juice, tofu, lemon juice, sweetener, cinnamon, vanilla, and cloves in blender and purée for 2 to 3 minutes or until very smooth, occasionally scraping down the sides of bowl. Scoop pudding into 4 small serving bowls or 4 wide-mouthed champagne glasses. Garnish with almonds (if using).

Makes 4 servings, 3/4 cup each

PER SERVING: calories 228, protein: 7 g, carbohydrate: 47 g, fat: 3 g, dietary fiber: 5 g, sodium: 39 mg

EXCELLENT SOURCE OF: vitamin C
GOOD SOURCE OF: calcium, iron, magnesium, potassium

% CALORIES FROM: protein 12%, fat 11%, carbohydrate 77%

Holiday Pie Topping

 This low-fat alternative to whipped cream is a great accompaniment to Pumpkin Pie (page 215), Blueberry Mince Tarts (page 203), or apple pie. It also can be served on its own as a creamy pudding; 1/2 cup serving is a good source of zinc.

12-ounce package firm silken tofu   1 tablespoon lemon juice

1/4 cup maple syrup   1 teaspoon vanilla extract

In blender or food processor, purée tofu, maple syrup, lemon juice, and vanilla for about 1 minute or until perfectly smooth. Chill for 1 to 2 hours. Spread over cooled pie or serve on each individual pie serving.

Makes 1 3/4 cups

PER 1/2 CUP: calories 125, protein: 7 g, carbohydrate: 19 g, fat: 3 g, dietary fiber: 0, sodium: 36 mg

GOOD SOURCE OF: zinc

% CALORIES FROM: protein 21%, fat 20%, carbohydrate 59%

Lemon Sesame Cookies

Thanks to Brenda Davis, dietitian, inspired baker, and speaker, for these exceptionally delectable cookies. They have a moist cake-like texture and lemon-sesame flavor. Serve them with a fresh fruit salad or pack them in your children's lunches or your own.

2 cups unbleached or all-purpose flour

1/2 cup sesame seeds

1/4 cup wheat germ

2 teaspoons baking powder

1/2 teaspoon salt

10–12 ounces soft tofu

1/2 cup maple syrup

1/2 cup canola or sunflower oil

1/4 cup Sucanat (page 219) or brown sugar

1 1/2 teaspoons lemon extract

1 teaspoon vanilla extract

1–2 teaspoons grated lemon peel

Preheat oven to 350°. Combine flour, sesame seeds, wheat germ, baking powder, and salt in bowl. In another bowl, mash tofu well. Stir in maple syrup, oil, Sucanat, lemon extract, vanilla, and lemon peel. Stir flour mixture into wet ingredients, mixing quickly. Drop by teaspoonfuls onto oiled baking sheet. Bake for about 12 minutes or until golden brown, rotating baking sheet after 5 to 7 minutes for even baking. Remove to rack to let cool. Store in covered jar or plastic container.

Makes 36 cookies

PER COOKIE: calories 79, protein: 2 g, carbohydrate: 9 g, fat: 4 g, dietary fiber: 0.9 g, sodium: 57 mg

% CALORIES FROM: protein 9%, fat 44%, carbohydrate 47%

Lem-Un-Cheesecake with Crumb Crust

 This pie can be made quickly from ingredients you keep on hand in your kitchen. You can use a commercial graham cracker crust or make the flavorful crumb crust given here. Once chilled, decorate the top of the cheesecake with fresh fruit such as strawberries, peaches, blueberries, or kiwis. Try serving this with Blueberry Orange Sauce (page 186).

Crumb Crust

This excellent crust was developed by Victoria Harrison, coauthor of *Becoming Vegetarian*. Ground flaxseed offers a nutty flavor and works best with Pumpkin Pie (page 215), whereas gluten flour provides a lighter taste and works best with the Lem-Un-Cheesecake.

I cup graham cracker crumbs or
   ground cereal (such as Nature's
   Path)
3/4 cup quick-cooking oat flakes
3 tablespoons gluten flour or
   ground flaxseed (see page 218)

1/4 cup canola oil
1/4 cup water
2 teaspoons vanilla extract

In bowl, stir together crumbs, oat flakes, and flaxseed. In small bowl, whisk together oil, water, and vanilla. Using fork, quickly stir oil mixture into crumb mixture. Using fingers, work oil mixture well into crumbs for a few seconds. Spray 9- or 10-inch pie plate with vegetable spray or coat lightly with oil. Press crumb mixture firmly and evenly onto sides and bottom of pie plate.

Filling

2 12-ounce packages firm silken
   tofu
1/3 cup maple syrup or honey

4 teaspoons grated lemon rind
1/4 cup lemon juice
1 1/2 teaspoons vanilla extract

Preheat oven to 350°. In food processor, purée tofu, maple syrup, lemon rind, lemon juice, and vanilla extract, occasionally scraping down sides of bowl. Pour mixture into unbaked pie shell and bake for 1 hour or until toothpick comes out clean and crust is beginning to set. Chill before serving.

Makes 8 servings

PER SERVING: calories 258, protein: 10 g, carbohydrate: 30 g, fat: 11 g, dietary fiber: 1 g, sodium: 124 mg
GOOD SOURCE OF: iron, magnesium, zinc, thiamin

% CALORIES FROM: protein 15%, fat 39%, carbohydrate 46%

No-Bake Chocolate Chews

 These fast and easy chocolate squares are a welcome treat for those with a sweet tooth. You may wish to use carob chips instead of chocolate chips.

1/2 cup almond or peanut butter

1/2 cup maple syrup, honey, or
  corn syrup

1/3 cup chocolate chips or 2.5 oz
  semisweet baking chocolate

1 teaspoon vanilla extract

2 cups crispy rice cereal or flaked
  cereal such as corn flakes

1/2 cup chopped unsalted
  almonds or walnuts

2 tablespoons wheat germ

Heat nut butter and maple syrup in pan over medium-high heat until nut butter softens and mixes easily with syrup. Lower heat to simmer and cook for 2 minutes, stirring constantly. Stir in chocolate chips until melted. Remove from heat and stir in vanilla. Mix in cereal, nuts, and wheat germ. Drop from teaspoon onto baking sheet lined with wax paper or pat into a lightly oiled 8-inch square cake pan. Refrigerate until firm.

Makes 24 squares

PER SQUARE: calories 89, protein: 2 g, carbohydrate: 10 g, fat: 5 g, dietary fiber: 0.7 g, sodium: 25 mg

% CALORIES FROM: protein 7%, fat 51%, carbohydrate 42%

Pumpkin Pie

This filling is adapted from a recipe developed by Mori-Nu Nutritional Foods, using their creamy smooth silken tofu. It can be baked in the Crumb Crust (page 212).

12-ounce package firm silken tofu

1 3/4 cups canned pumpkin
  (15 oz) or 2 cups cooked

2/3 cup maple syrup or honey

1 teaspoon vanilla extract

1 1/2 teaspoons ground cinnamon

3/4 teaspoon ground ginger

1/4 teaspoon ground nutmeg

1/8–1/4 teaspoon ground cloves

Unbaked Crumb Crust (page 212)

Preheat oven to 375°. Blend tofu in a food processor or blender until creamy smooth. Add pumpkin, maple syrup, vanilla, cinnamon, ginger, nutmeg, and cloves; blend well. Pour into Crumb Crust and bake for 50 to 60 minutes or until pie just begins to crack.

Makes 8 servings (although on one occasion Joseph ate the whole pie all by himself—it's that good!)

PER 1/8 PIE, WITH CRUST: calories 306, protein: 7 g, carbohydrate: 43 g, fat: 12 g, dietary fiber: 5 g, sodium: 134 mg

EXCELLENT SOURCE OF: vitamin A
GOOD SOURCE OF: iron, zinc, thiamin

% CALORIES FROM: protein 10%, fat 34%, carbohydrate 56%

Vegan Dass Ice Cream

 If you have a food processor, a Green Power juice extractor, or a Champion juicer, you can make the simplest, lowest-fat, nondairy ice cream imaginable. All you do is freeze some bananas overnight on a tray or in a plastic bag and then take a few minutes to process them into a smooth dessert. The nutritional analysis is exceptional, because the only ingredient is bananas! After you try the basic recipe, experiment with some of your own variations such as adding some carob, chocolate powder, blueberries, or strawberries.

4 bananas, peeled, broken into quarters, and frozen

Place bananas in food processor of choice and process until smooth.

VARIATIONS: For a sorbet-type frozen dessert, use a few frozen strawberries or raspberries, mango, pineapple, or kiwi. Try a ratio of 2 frozen bananas to 1 cup of other frozen fruit.

Makes 4 servings

PER SERVING: calories 109, protein: 1 g, carbohydrate: 28 g, fat: 0.6 g, dietary fiber: 3 g, sodium: 1 mg

GOOD SOURCE OF: potassium (bananas are famous as potassium sources!)

% CALORIES FROM: protein 4 %, fat 4%, carbohydrate 92%

Appendix One

Making Friends with New Ingredients

Several ingredients used in many of our recipes need to be introduced so you are comfortable with their use. Our goal is for you to become familiar with these ingredients and to use them in good health.

Agar

Agar, also known as agar-agar, is a white to pale yellow extract from a species of red seaweed. Once processed it is sold as a powder, flakes, or bars. Agar has valuable characteristics such as its ability to gel liquids at a wide range of pH and temperatures, making it an excellent vegetarian replacement for gelatin (which is derived from the bones and hooves of cattle and horses). It also acts as a flavor fixative, thus helping lock in flavor from other ingredients. Agar is readily available at larger health food markets and is very inexpensive at Oriental stores.

Since agar powder, flakes, and bars differ considerably due to their respective densities, care must be taken to use the product called for in a recipe. For instance, if you were to use agar powder instead of flakes, your end product would likely resemble a hockey puck since the powder is much denser than the flakes. (We discovered that the hard way.) If flakes were used instead of powder, the product would not have sufficient gel.

Guidelines

Agar needs to be thoroughly dissolved in liquid for it to gel. Agar bars may be crumbled into flakes before measuring.

Thickening power may vary from one brand of agar to another. This is generally a function of quality. If you find that the amount of agar called for results in too soft or too firm a product, take note and make the appropriate adjustment for your next attempt.

- ♦ 1 tablespoon of agar flakes will thicken 1 cup of fruit juice
- ♦ 1/2 teaspoon of agar powder will thicken 1 cup of juice

Flaxseed

Flaxseeds, also known as linseeds, are reddish-brown oval seeds, slightly bigger than sesame seeds. The soluble fiber present in ground flaxseed attracts and holds liquid. Due to this characteristic, a tablespoon of ground flaxseed, mixed with water, gives a binding quality similar to that provided by an egg. It is an excellent cholesterol-free egg replacer for use in baked items and helps to produce a moist, light product. Flaxseed can be purchased ground or you can grind whole seeds in your blender or small spice/coffee grinder. Whole flaxseeds do not require refrigeration, however ground flaxseed should be stored in the freezer to prevent the omega-3 fatty acids that are exposed to air from becoming rancid. Uncooked ground flaxseed is high in essential omega-3 fatty acids.

Flaxseed as an egg replacer
One tablespoon of ground flaxseed plus 3 tablespoons of water is equivalent to one egg. Mix ground flaxseed and water in a small bowl and let sit for 1 to 2 minutes. Add to recipe for pancakes, muffins, or other baked goods, as you would add an egg.

Flaxseed oil
Flaxseed oil is approximately 57 percent by weight, omega-3 fatty acids (linolenic acid). Flaxseed oil must be stored in your refrigerator or freezer and should not be heated. Heat will destroy the inherent goodness. This precious oil has a strong initial taste, but many people report that after using it for a while the oil has a buttery taste.

Nutritional Yeast

Nutritional yeast is a dietary supplement and condiment, rich in B vitamins. It has a distinct cheese-like flavor and a pleasant aroma. Although there are many brands of nutritional yeast powder or flakes, the Red Star Vegetarian Support Formula is recommended because it is a primary product grown on a vitamin B12-rich medium. This makes it a reliable source of vitamin B12 for vegans. Nutritional yeast is not a leavening agent. It can be found at health food stores in bulk or in packages.

Sucanat

Sucanat is an acronym for SUgar CAne NATural. It is a wholesome, tasty, golden brown granular sugar derived from certified organic cane juice. Vitamins, minerals, and trace minerals naturally found in the sugar cane plant are retained, as only the moisture is removed. The molasses is what gives Sucanat its delicious characteristic flavor. It may be used as a more nutritious one-for-one replacement for white, refined, or brown sugar.

Soybeans

In China, soybeans are known as *ta tou,* the greater bean, and with good reason. Soybeans have been highly valued in the Orient for thousands of years, due to the outstanding qualities of their protein and oil and to their versatility. In recent times, North American scientists have discovered the excellent amino acid profile of soybeans and recognized that highly digestible soyfoods such as tofu are first rate when protein sources are compared, whether plant or animal. The plant oils in soy are also good sources of essential omega-3 fatty acids. In addition, considerable research is being done on the health benefits of isoflavones in soy. These beneficial phytochemicals function as antioxidants and as mild plant estrogens. Add soy to your diet and you may lower your risk of heart disease, certain cancers, and osteoporosis; for women, the severity of menopausal symptoms may be reduced.

Soy Milk

Soy milk, which is required to be described on its label as a "soy beverage," is prepared by washing, soaking, grinding, and cooking soybeans. The fibrous part of the mash, called okara, is removed, and the remaining soy milk is packaged with or without added flavoring.

The flavors of different brands vary considerably. You'll probably find some you don't particularly like and others you really enjoy. Those soy milks with "soy protein" or "soy protein isolate" on the ingredient list are prepared by a series of steps in which fractions of the whole soybean are extracted, often using acids, alkalis, and the solvent hexane. You may prefer instead to use a soy beverage that is made from whole soybeans. You'll also be making a good investment by choosing organic non-genetically engineered products and selecting a soy milk that is fortified with calcium, zinc, and vitamins D and B12.

Tofu: many textures, many uses

In the process of making tofu, hot soy milk is blended with a coagulant to form a curd. At this stage, soft-grade tofu is poured directly into its package. Soft tofu tends to be relatively high in water and low in protein and minerals compared with the firmer varieties. The coagulant was traditionally a seaweed extract called nigari, however modern processes often use magnesium or calcium salts; the latter can make it a good source of calcium (read the Nutrition Information panel on the package).

For medium, firm, and extra-firm grades of tofu, the curd is poured into a mold, covered with cotton, pressed to form a block, cut, and then packaged. The amount of pressure applied and water expelled determines whether the tofu will be medium, firm, or extra firm in consistency. Since the texture varies for each of these types, they each have specific uses in recipes. As blocks of tofu vary considerably, our recipes describe tofu in weight measures. When making your purchase, please read the label for weight.

Why recipes call for "pressed medium tofu"

The smoothness of the medium tofu is of value in many recipes; however, the water content may still be too high for certain recipes such as Curry Sandwich Spread (page 74) and Scrambled Tofu (page 69). If the tofu in these recipes were used without first pressing out excess water, the liquid would "weep" into the bread or onto the serving plate.

How to press medium tofu

Remove tofu from package and place it on a baking pan. Over the tofu, place another pan or a cutting board, and on that carefully place a 4- or 5-pound weight, such as two or three cans of tomato sauce or a telephone book. Press the tofu for 15 to 20 minutes. Approximately 1/2 cup of liquid will have pooled in the bottom pan; it can be discarded. Transfer the tofu to a bowl and proceed with the recipe.

Silken tofu

Silken tofu, of Japanese origin, is particularly silky in nature. Like other (Chinese) tofu on the market, it ranges from soft to extra firm. Silken tofu is poured directly into an aseptic box and needs no refrigeration before opening. It's handy for camping trips and to keep on the shelf for use when company arrives and you'd like to make a Lem-Un-Cheesecake (page 212) or Pumpkin Pie (page 215). Mori Nu Silken Tofu is the most widely sold and comes in 12.3-ounce packages.

Cereal Grains—The Staff of Life

The use of cereal grains can be traced back to the dawn of civilization. From earliest times, tribes focused their attention on primitive agricultural techniques that centered around growing cereal grasses. With time, particular grains became associated with specific regions and cultural groups. Many nations of the world have a cereal that can be traced to their origins. The Russians have buckwheat, the Chinese and Japanese have rice, the Scottish and Irish have oats, Central America has corn and the great plains of Canada and the United States have wheat and rye.

Grains, the small fruit or kernel of cereal grasses, are the edible seeds of those grasses. What has made them so important in the history of the world is their nutritional composition. Grains are made up of four distinct parts, with protein distributed throughout all four. The first layer is the husk, also known as the chaff. The chaff is the tough protective layer that surrounds the fruit and keeps it protected from the natural elements during its growth. The husk is indigestible for humans and once removed, it is discarded.

The next part is the bran. This layer surrounds the seed and is rich in vitamins, minerals, and fiber, both soluble and insoluble. The thin bran layer surrounds the endosperm, the biggest part of the grain, which stores most of the kernel's food energy in the form of complex carbohydrate.

A tiny but very important portion of the grain is the germ or embryo. This is the center of life or germination, a portion that abounds with vitamins, minerals, and essential fatty acids. Unfortunately, this fraction of the seed, along with the bran, is removed in the milling and refining process, as its oils can become rancid during storage. In the case of wheat, for example, this refining results in a pure-looking white product that has a longer shelf life. However, even when three of the B vitamins (niacin, riboflavin, and thiamin) and iron are added back in the enrichment process, white flour has lost much of the vitamins (folate, vitamin B$_6$), minerals (chromium, magnesium, and zinc), fiber, and essential fatty acids.

In North America and Europe, grains such as oatmeal and flaked and puffed cereals have primarily been associated with breakfast. However, many delicious and distinctively-flavored grains can take a central place at lunch and dinner, as they do around the world. The grains used in the majority of our recipes are unrefined for maximum nutrition.

General guidelines for cooking grains

The size of pot used for cooking cereal grains is important. For small quantities, a small deep pot ensures that the grain is covered by liquid for as long as possible before it absorbs all of the liquid. When cooking grains, the lid should be tight-fitting, since all the liquid needs to be absorbed and evaporation needs to be kept to a minimum.

Generally speaking, grains take less time to cook than legumes, and do not require presoaking. Always bring water to a boil before adding grains. (Cold water will draw some of the starch from grains into the surrounding water. When grains are added to the water before bringing to a boil, the starch slightly thickens the water, resulting in a sticky final product. This is particularly true for grains that have had the bran removed, such as white basmati rice.) Once the water has come to a boil, add the grain, cover the pot, and wait for the water to return to boil before reducing the heat to simmer.

The matter of whether to add salt to the cooking water is a personal choice. As a rule of thumb, salt the water (if using salt) before the grains are added to the pot. This allows the grain an opportunity to absorb the salt as it cooks.

Grains are cooked when all the water has been absorbed and when the grain is soft and no longer crunchy. If the cooking temperature is too high and too much water has been lost through evaporation, add a small amount of hot water to the pot to complete the cooking. Do not stir the grains while they are cooking or immediately afterwards, while the grain is hot. Grains bruise very easily and stirring will make them sticky. Once the grain is cooked, allow the pot to rest for 5 minutes off the heat before serving. If any moisture remains on the bottom of the pot, drain it off.

Some grains will undoubtedly suit your liking more than others and will become staples in your household. Since grains have slightly different nutritional profiles, eating a variety ensures a range of nutrient intake.

The Cooking Times for Grains chart below is based on 1 cup of raw grain. Generally speaking, 1 cup of dry grain will yield 2 servings; however, this depends on how hungry the eaters are and the amounts of other foods served. Leftover grains can be easily reheated or incorporated into soups, salads, International Roll-Ups (page 139) and grain puddings.

Cooking Times for Grains (based on cooking 1 cup of raw grain)

GRAIN	ADDED WATER	COOKING TIME	YIELD
Amaranth	1 1/2 cups	25 min.	2 cups
Barley, pearl	4 cups	50–60 min.	4 cups
Buckwheat	2 cups	12–15 min.	4 cups
Bulgur, medium grind	2 1/2 cups	let stand 20–30 min.	3 cups
Cornmeal, yellow	4 cups	5–10 min.	4 1/2 cups
Millet	2 1/2 cups	25 min.	4 cups
Oats, quick-cooking	2 cups	2–3 min.	2 1/4 cups
Oats, rolled	2 1/2 cups	20 min.	2 1/4 cups
Quinoa	1 1/2 cups	15–20 min.	3 1/2 cups
Rice, brown basmati	2 cups	40 min.	3 1/4 cups
Rice, brown short grain	2 cups	45 min.	3 1/2 cups
Rice, brown long grain	2 cups	45 min.	3 1/2 cups
Rice, white basmati	1 3/4 cups	18–20 min.	3 cups
Wheat berries	3 1/2 cups	50–60 min.	3 cups
Wild rice, whole	4 cups	50–60 min.	3 cups

Legumes: Plant Powerhouses

Legumes form the second most important source of food to humans, after cereal grains. Plants with seeds in pods and the seeds of those pods are known as legumes. These highly nutritious edible seeds are the protein powerhouses of the plant kingdom.

Why presoak beans and peas?

When beans are harvested they have a high percentage of moisture. Bringing beans to market requires that they be dried to prolong shelf life. Once dried, beans can be stored for years, in fact legumes that would still germinate were found in the tombs of the pharaohs. Soaking overnight reconstitutes beans to that point when they were harvested and considerably reduces their cooking time.

In addition, soaking draws out of the legumes some of the carbohydrates (oligosaccharides) that are not digested well in the small intestine. These carbohydrates pass through to the large intestine, where they are acted upon by naturally occurring bacteria. A byproduct of this bacterial activity is intestinal gas, which in excessive amounts, can produce discomfort in the lower bowel and be embarrassing. Discarding the soaking liquid and rinsing beans before they are cooked goes a long way towards reducing intestinal gas. For further information on this topic turn to "The Gas Crisis: International Solutions" in Chapter 7 of *Becoming Vegetarian* (The Book Publishing Company).

When legumes are soaked, their minerals become more available for our use. Calcium, iron, and zinc are released from a phosphate complex known as phytate, allowing more of these minerals to be absorbed by the body. Thus, more nutritional value is extracted from presoaked beans than from beans that are cooked from a dry state.

Small beans such as mung beans, peas, and lentils do not have to be soaked before cooking. Their smaller size allows them to cook more quickly than the larger beans such as kidney or garbanzo beans (also called chick-peas). If you have the time and wish to capitalize on the increased mineral availability that soaking produces, by all means soak the small legumes as well before cooking them.

Depending on the source of the legumes you buy, you may need to pick them over before soaking to remove any twigs, pieces of dirt, or small stones from the field. To do this, spread them unto a baking sheet and remove unwanted bits. If you travel abroad, to Nepal or India for example, you will see women sitting together sociably and doing this task between meals. If peas or lentils are not going to be presoaked, rinse them to remove any dust.

A general rule of thumb for soaking legumes is to cover them with triple their volume of water for at least 6 hours or overnight. Legumes will expand between 2 and 3 times their dried volume, so make sure the bowl or pot you use is large enough.

Quick-Soaking Procedure

If you haven't soaked legumes, you can still salvage your plans to have beans for dinner. Rinse the beans and place them in a pot. Add triple the amount of water, bring to a boil, cover, reduce the heat to low, and simmer for 5 minutes. Remove the pot from heat and let rest for 1 hour. Then cook according to the directions below.

General Cooking Guidelines

Discard the soaking or rinsing liquid and cover with triple the amount of fresh cold water. Bring the legumes to boil in a covered pot, then reduce the heat to simmer. Simmering the legumes is important, as boiling reduces the water too quickly and also bursts the skins. Some legumes produce a foam in the water after it comes to a boil. Skim off the foam once or twice using a slotted spoon or ladle. The remaining foam will eventually disappear. Keep the pot lid tilted slightly to the side to prevent the water from spilling over and allow steam to escape. If the water does reduce before the legumes are cooked, simply add a bit more to cover the beans by 1/2 inch. Return the lid to the tilted position and continue cooking.

Do not add salt at the beginning of the cooking process. Salt and acidic products such as tomatoes, wine, vinegar, citrus juices, and sweeteners toughen the outer skin of legumes. This makes it more difficult for water to penetrate the legume and thus increases the cooking time. Legumes are cooked when they are no longer crunchy when bitten. Test a few as some may be cooked before others.

Let the beans cool in their cooking liquid. This keeps their skins from splitting as a result of coming into contact with the cooler air.

Is salt needed when cooking beans?

This depends on your preference. Adding a small amount of salt (1/4 teaspoon) toward the end of cooking develops the overall flavor of legumes and decreases the need for salt when adjusting the final seasoning.

Do mountain dwellers need to cook beans longer?

Yes; at sea level, the boiling point of water is 212° and at higher elevations the boiling point is lower, thus requiring more time to cook and bake.

Cooking Times for Legumes

All yields are based on 1 cup of raw legumes and 3 cups of cooking water and reflect a 6-hour soaking time, except where noted. Note that cooking times vary considerably depending on the length of soaking time, age, size, and variety of the legume. (Older beans take longer to cook.)

BEAN	MINIMUM COOKING TIME	APPROXIMATE YIELD
aduki beans	60 min. (90 min. unsoaked)	3 cups
black beans	55 min.	2 1/2 cups
black-eyed peas	60 min.	2 cups
garbanzo beans/chick-peas	60 min.	2 1/2 cups
great northern beans	60 min.	2 2/3 cups
kidney beans	45 min.	2 2/3 cups
lentils, brown	20 min. (45 min. unsoaked)	2 1/2 cups
lentils, red	15–20 min. (unsoaked)	2 cups
lima beans, small	60 min.	2 1/2 cups
mung beans	25–30 min. (40–50 min. unsoaked)	3 cups
navy beans	75 min.	2 2/3 cups
pinto beans	45 min.	2 2/3 cups
split peas	45–60 min. (unsoaked)	2 cups

Appendix Two

Sources of Ingredients and Equipment

The following companies provide high-quality natural foods, ingredients, and equipment that we use in our kitchens. We recommend that you investigate these companies and begin incorporating their products into your cooking.

Almond Board of California, 1150 Ninth Street, Suite 1500, Modesto, California 94354; Phone: 209/549-8262, ext. 114; Fax: 209/549-8267; www.almondsarein.com

Annie's of Vermont, Foster Hill Road, North Calais, Vermont 05650 Phone: 802/456-8866; Fax: 802/456-8865—Makers of great tasting, low-fat barbecue sauce and excellent salad dressings.

Bob's Red Mill, 5209 S.E. International Way, Milwaukee, Oregon 97222; Phone: 503/654-3215; Fax: 503/653-1339—An incredible array of packaged ground grains, beans, seeds, pancake mixes, and more. Flours are ground with a 4,000-pound stone. Also amidst the selection of products are xanthan gum, specialty beans, cereals, lecithin granules…the list goes on. Top quality and delicious.

California Fig Advisory Board, 3425 North First Street, Suite 109, Fresno, California 93726; Phone: 800/588-2344; Fax: 209/244-3449

Eden Foods, 701 Tecumseh Road, Clinton, Michigan 49236; Phone: 800/248-0301 or 517/456-7424; Fax: 517/456-7025; www.eden-foods.com—Eden Foods is a natural food manufacturer, trader, and contract grower of organically grown and traditional food. About 130 excellent Eden brand products, including hijiki, nori, and agar seaweed products, Eden Organic Pasta, beans, tomatoes, rice syrup, toasted sesame oil, and exceptional imported foods are sold throughout the United States.

Frontier Cooperative Herbs, 3021 78th Street, Norway, Iowa 52318; Phone: 800/786-1388—Member-owned since 1976, Frontier is a manufacturer and supplier of natural and organic products that include non-irradiated herbs and spices, organic coffee, tea, natural remedies, and aromatherapy goods.

Green Power Juice Extractor, Green Power International, 12020 Woodruff Ave., Suite C, Dowdney, California; Phone: 888/254-7336 or 310/940-4241; Fax: 310/940-4240—This juicer can produce not only the superb Vegan Dass Ice Cream on page 216, but also fruit and vegetable juices that retain top nutritional quality as well as baby food, nut butters, and pasta.

Imagine Foods, 350 Cambridge Avenue, Suite 350, Palo Alto, California 94306; Phone: 415/327-1444—Imagine Foods specializes in vegan and nondairy products derived from rice, including: Rice Dream Beverage, yummy Rice Dream Frozen Desserts, and Imagine Pudding Snacks. Imagine also offers Ken and Robert's Veggie Pockets—hand-held vegetarian entrées in an organic crust, available in ten international flavors.

Lundberg Family Farms, 5370 Church Street, Richvale, California 95974-0369; Phone: 916/882-4551; Fax: 916/882-4500—Rice and rice products such as entrées, cereals, puddings, rice cakes, and rice syrups. Lundberg Family Farms' growing and processing techniques have developed out of the family's deep rooted beliefs about the land and surrounding ecology.

Mori-Nu Tofu, 2050 W. 190th Street, Suite 110, Torrence, California 90504; Phone: 800/NOW-TOFU or 310/787-0200; Fax: 310/787-2727; Home page: http://www.morinu.com—This company provides the excellent Mori Nu silken tofu that was used to develop recipes throughout this book. Both regular and lite are available; we prefer the regular, which is highest in isoflavones. Mori-Nu's revolutionary aseptic package keeps this tofu fresh without refrigeration, preservatives, or irradiation for months. Its versatile, creamy, smooth texture provides a plant protein alternative to milk, cream, cheese, and eggs in thousands of recipes. It's handy for camping trips, too!

Muir Glen Organic Tomato Products, 424 North 7th Street, Sacramento, California 95814; Phone: 800/832-6345; Fax: 916/557-0903—Muir Glen Organic Tomato Products are grown in accordance with the California Organic Foods Act of 1990. They offer a full line of canned organic tomato products, including juice, ketchup, sauce, diced, ground peeled, and whole peeled tomatoes, plus a full line of jar-packed pasta sauces and salsas. All their products are packed in either lead-free, enamel-lined, recyclable cans or recyclable clear glass jars.

Nature's Path/LifeStream, 7453 Progress Way, Delta, British Columbia V4G 1E8; Phone: 604/940-0505; Fax: 604/940-0522; E-mail: cereal@ naturespath.bc.ca—Nature's Path products are 100 percent organic and certified kosher. The product line consists of an excellent range of flaked cereals (boxed and EcoPacs) and muesli. LifeStream produces frozen waffles.

Omega Nutrition USA Inc., 6515 Aldrich Road, Bellingham, Washington 98226; Phone: 800/661-3529; Fax: 604/253-4228; E-mail: omega @istar.ca; Web: http://www.omegaflo.com—Manufacturer of fresh pressed, unrefined, certified organic flaxseed oil, garlic-chili flaxseed oil, olive oil, safflower oil, coconut oil, sesame oil, canola oil, and sunflower oil. Other refined oils include hazelnut, pistachio, and pumpkin, as well as Essential Balance and Essential Balance Jr., the five oil blends that provide a 1:1 ratio of omega-3 and omega-6 essential fatty acids. Omega also carries unfiltered, unpasteurized apple cider vinegar (Oregon Tilth Certified Organic) and much more. All products are packaged in light- and oxygen-proof containers to preserve freshness.

ProSoya Foods Incorporated, 15350 56th Ave, Surrey, British Columbia V3S 8E7; Phone: 604/576-8038, ext. 35 for product information; Fax: 604/576-6037; E-mail: ipc@direct.ca—ProSoya So Nice soy beverages and soy yogurt stand out for their exceptionally good taste and top quality ingredients, including organic and non-genetically engineered soybeans. Four flavors of the beverages—original, vanilla, chocolate, and cappuccino—are fortified with calcium, zinc, riboflavin, and vitamins B12, D, and A. "Natural" is unfortified. The soy yogurt comes in four fruit flavors and vanilla.

Red Star Yeast & Products, Division of Universal Foods Corporation, P.O. Box 737, Milwaukee, Wisconsin 53202; Phone: 800/558-9892 or 414/271-6755—Producers of Vegetarian Support Formula, a nutritional yeast product. Vegetarian Support Formula contains B vitamins, including a reliable source of natural vitamin B12 and was developed specifically for vegetarians, due to the need for a reliable B12 source. This product may be used to enhance the flavor and nutritional value of meals and snacks.

Santa Barbara Olive Co. Inc., P.O. Box 1570, 3280 Calrada Rd., Santa Ynez, California 93460; Phone: 805/688-9917; Fax: 805/686-1659— This company boasts eight generations in horticulture and viticulture in Santa Barbara, California and excellent certified Organic olives.

Sucanat North American Corporation, 525 Fentress Blvd., Daytona Beach Florida 32120; Phone: 800/860-1896; Fax: 904/947-4707; E-mail: sucanat@aol.com—SUgar CAne NATural is a tasty golden brown sugar derived from 100 PERCENT evaporated cane juice made from freshly squeezed sugar cane juice. Because nothing is added and only water is removed, Sucanat retains the vitamins, minerals, and trace elements found naturally in the sugar cane plant. Sucanat may be used as a one-for-one replacement for white, refined, or brown sugar.

Yves Veggie Cuisine, 1638 Derwent Way, Delta, British Columbia V3M 6R9; Phone: 604/525-1345; Fax: 604/525-2555; www.yvesveggie.com— Yves Veggie Cuisine manufactures a full line of tasty, nutritious, and easy-to-prepare food products that are made from vegetable protein. They are low in saturated fat, cholesterol free, and contain no preservatives or artificial ingredients. The company's product line includes wieners, burgers, patties, slices, vegetarian ground round, veggie pepperoni, and breakfast links.

Appendix Three

 Selected References and Resources

References

Becoming Vegetarian, 1995, by Vesanto Melina, Brenda Davis, and Victoria Harrison, The Book Publishing Company. http://home.ican. net/~melina

Diet, Nutrition and Prevention of Chronic Diseases, 1991 World Health Organization Study Group on Diet, Nutrition and Prevention of Non-communicable Diseases. Geneva, Switzerland Technical Report Series No. 797. World Health Organization.

Eco-Cuisine, 1995; and *Friendly Foods,* 1991, by Ron Pickarski, Ten Speed Press, Berkeley, CA. http://eco-cuisine.com

Dr. Dean Ornish's Program for Reversing Heart Disease, 1990, Ballantine Books; *Eat More, Weigh Less,* by Dr. Dean Ornish, 1993, HarperPerennial; *Everyday Cooking with Dr. Dean Ornish,* 1996, HarperCollins.

Famous Vegetarians and Their Favorite Recipes, 1996, and *Food for the Gods, Vegetarianism and the World's Religions,* 1998, by Rynn Berry, Pythagorean Publishers, New York, NY.

"Plant Proteins in Relation to Human Protein and Amino Acid Nutrition," 1994, Young, V.R. and Pellett, P.L. *American Journal of Clinical Nutrition,* volume 59 (supplement), pages 1203S-1212S.

Surgeon General's Report on Nutrition and Health, U.S. Department of Health and Human Services. http://muu.lib.hel.fi/McSpotlight/media/reports/surgen_rep.html

The Gathering Place, 1997, by Graham Kerr, plus 22 more cookbook titles, which have sold more than 14 million copies.

The Moosewood Cookbook, 1977, Mollie Katzen, Ten Speed Press, Berkeley, CA.

Table for Two, 1996, and *The Uncheese Cookbook,* 1994, Joanne Stepaniak, The Book Publishing Co.

Resources

American Vegan Society—609/694-2887

North American Vegetarian Society—518/568-7970; http://www.cyberveg.org/navs/

The Vegetarian Resource Group—410/366-VEGE; http://www.vrg.org/

Position of The American Dietetic Association: Vegetarian Diets— http://www.eatright.org/adap1197.html

Physicians Committee for Responsible Medicine—202/686-2110; http://www.pcrm.org; pcrm@prcm.org

See page 40 for references and resources used for nutritional analysis.

Index